ANGELS LONG TO SEE THESE THINGS

Mankind's Past - Present – Future

Trish Lord

This book is affectionately dedicated to my sons Tony and Nathan and my grandsons Noah, Caleb & Ezra.

It is my prayer that you will realize the certainty of God's plan for humanity and for you individually and that God's purpose will be your passion. Then you will find your God given destiny. The joy and peace that surpasses all understanding will be yours.

This knowledge will allow you to make a difference in a world that is lost and in the eternity that is to come.

CONTENTS

A FUTURE AGE AND TIME

*Jerusalem, Israel in the year 237
of the thousand year reign of Jesus Christ.*

We are all gathered for the annual Feast of Tabernacles, a festival God established thousands of years ago. This is a time of great celebration for every person living on earth. Here in Israel, everyone comes to Jerusalem to hear the reading of God's plan for mankind. We gather to hear this story throughout our lives as a constant reminder of mankind's past, present, and future. The annual festival is also a time when we celebrate the thousand year reign of Christ on Earth. It has been two hundred and thirty seven years since Jesus began His Theocratic Kingdom. On this day, people from every nation come together to rejoice for all of the great things which have happened since the Messiah began ruling over all nations and people of the world.

Thousands of years of spiritual conflict between humans and Satan ended with the Second Coming of Christ. Satan and all of his demons were bound for one thousand years and prohibited from influencing humans. Because Jesus Christ is our King, divine righteousness is displayed over all the earth. All outward sources of temptation from demons have been removed from us. We now live in an age of peace and comfort unlike any other time in mankind's history. It's hard to imagine that in seven hundred and sixty three years the seal that holds Satan in the Abyss will be broken and he must be released for a short time. When he returns his ultimate goal will be to bring as many people to hell with him as he possibly can through deception. The Word of God tells us at the end of this Millennium, Satan will deceive many people. However, God's plan for mankind, revealed through His Word, gives everyone the knowledge and understanding necessary to fight and win the ongoing battle between the forces of good and evil. It has been this way since the Bible was written; never changing and giving divine guidance and wisdom to all who read it throughout the ages.

As I gaze into the enormous fire, I find myself hypnotized by the flickering lights dancing on top of the wood. I see thousands of anxious faces, old and young, that are illuminated from the firelight. Suddenly a voice begins speaking. Immediately, the crowd quiets and the story begins....

Part One

IN THE BEGINNING

Chapter One

ANOTHER PLACE–
ANOTHER TIME

❧

B eyond the limits of time and space, in a place of another dimension called heaven, God the Father, God the Son and God the Holy Spirit fashioned the universe. Within the universe, at just the perfect place, God would create a planet designed to sustain life forms. One of these life forms would be made in His very image. This being would live in a body that required particular physical conditions in order to survive. God's creation would be uniquely designed.

God is love. He wanted to create a people He could reach out to with His love, and receive love back. God wanted relationship with humans. God's plan for the universe, the earth and for humanity began to unfold.

In the beginning God created the heavens and the earth. The earth was formless and empty, and darkness covered the deep waters. And the Spirit of God was hovering over the surface of the waters. (Genesis 1: 1-2)

Then God said "Let there be light" and he separated the light from the darkness and called them day and night. God made the firmament and separated the waters and called the firmament heavens. Then He collected the water into one place and the dry land appeared and he called the dry land Earth and the waters Seas. God put vegetation, plants and trees on the earth. He turned his attention to the heavens and put lights in the expanse to separate the day from the night and to mark seasons, days and years. He placed the sun and the moon and stars in the heavens to give light on the earth. God created multitudes of various creatures and birds and blessed them saying, "Be fruitful, multiply, and fill the waters in the seas and multiply in the earth."

God included three different heavens in His creation. Two of the heavens were placed around planet earth and the third is above the others where He lives. The heaven directly around the earth is called the firmament or the first heaven. The second heaven is in between heaven where God lives and the earth-realm; it is called the heavenlies.

The third heaven is the most glorious place in the universe. The temple of God is located there and His throne sits in the inner court of the temple. The radiance from the glory of God in His might and power creates great bursts of light flashing forth from Him like a glittering diamond, or a shining ruby. The throne has a rainbow, resembling an emerald encircling it. Surrounding the throne are twenty-four other thrones. Seated on these are twenty-four celestial beings. They are dressed in white and have crowns of gold on their heads. Directly in front of the throne are seven lighted lamps and a golden altar with four horns. Spread out before the altar is a magnificent sea of glass as clear as crystal. In the center around His throne, are four celestial beings whose task it is to guard the throne and worship God. Each of these creatures has six wings with the central sections of their wings covered with eyes. Nothing escapes their attention!

Angels

God created heavenly beings called angels that dwell in the third heaven with Him. They are celestial, spirit beings that live eternally. Angels are numbered in the multitudes and hold an exalted place in the royal order of God's creation. There are several orders of angels who have different degrees of authority and celestial powers. They all possess a great amount of knowledge, power and mobility and are not confined by time, space, or matter. These celestial beings have the ability to travel through time and dimensions. Angels also have the capability of appearing and disappearing in the time it takes to blink an eye. Angels do not possess physical bodies, unless God assigns them to a special mission which requires them to take on a physical form. Angels cannot reproduce and they do not marry. They speak, think, feel have free will, and emotions. Angels are primarily ministering spirits, messengers and sent as agents to carry out God's orders in the universe. They are a very organized, massive group of angelic powers who are a very significant part of God's great plan for mankind. Tens of thousands of angels encircle God's throne singing and making music of celebration to the glory of God.

Archangels are chief princes in the divine order of angels. One archangel named Michael is the great prince of heaven who has been given enormous authority, a special guardian who protects God's creation. He is a very powerful angel who commands armies of angels into battle when necessary.

There was another angel named Lucifer, the most brilliant and magnificent of all created beings in heaven. He was a ruling prince in the universe, a servant of God. Lucifer was the director of praise and worship and led great choruses of angels in glorious adoration of God. Lucifer was perfect in beauty and full of wisdom.

Gabriel is another angel who holds a very high office in the order established by God. He is primarily a messenger unfolding the plans, purposes and verdicts of God. There are also angels called seraphim and cherubim. The seraphim are six winged creatures full of eyes around and within them. These beautiful angelic beings are positioned above God's throne and do not rest day or night. Angelic beings are constantly giving glory, honor and thanks to God. The cherubim are positioned beside God's throne and like the seraphim faithfully worship God. They have wings, feet and hands. Seraphim and cherubim are incredibly exquisite, powerful, majestic creatures. They perform the task of guarding over the holy places of God. Massive amounts of angels witnessed the dazzling show, as God created the earth, heavens and mankind.

Mankind

On the sixth day God created mankind in His own image. He formed man out of the dust of the ground and then breathed into his nostrils the breath of life and he became a living being.

> *Then God said, "Let Us make human beings in our image, to be like us. They will reign over the fish in the sea, the birds in the sky, the livestock, all the wild animals on the earth, and the small animals that scurry along the ground." So God created human beings in his own image. In the image of God He created them; male and female he created them. (Genesis 1:26-27)*

God planted a garden eastward in a place called Eden, the most spectacular site imaginable filled with beauty beyond compare. Man was placed in the world like a king in a palace. Everyday God came down to the garden and fellowshipped with the man he named Adam and woman He called Eve. They shared their love for one another and had a wonderful relationship together. Often they walked and talked enjoying each other's company in this splendid garden God had created for them to delight in. This garden with all of its creatures and physical features was so amazingly beautiful that God's glory shined brilliantly everywhere they looked.

The tree of life and the tree of the knowledge of the difference between good and evil were in the center of the garden. He gave Adam and Eve a very specific command with a warning that disobedience would bring a severe consequence.

> But the Lord God warned him, "You may freely eat the fruit of every tree in the garden- except the tree of the knowledge of good and evil. If you eat its fruit, you are sure to die." (Genesis 2: 16-17)

Rebellion in Heaven

Back in the realm of the third heaven, Lucifer became filled with pride, because of his great beauty and wisdom. He desired praise and adoration for himself. He thought he should be exhalted like God and he wanted to rule over heaven and creation in God's place. Wanting what did not belong to him, he sought supreme authority. Lucifer was consumed with wickedness and pride and the spirit of rebellion overtook this angel. He planned a revolution against God and cleverly persuaded some of the other angels in heaven to join him in this great act of defiance. Many of the other angels also denied the authority of God and joined Lucifer in his war.

"You were the perfection of wisdom and exquisite in beauty. You were in Eden, the garden of God. Your clothing was adorned with every precious stone- red carnelian, chrysolite, white moonstone, beryl, onyx, jasper, sapphire, turquoise, and emerald- all beautifully crafted for you and set in the finest gold. They were given to you on the day you were created. I ordained and anointed you as the mighty angelic guardian. You had access to the holy mountain of God and walked among the stones of fire. You were blameless in all you did from the day you were created until the day evil was found in you." (Ezekiel 28: 12-15)

The first great catastrophe in the history of creation was Lucifer's defiance of God's authority. Because of rebellion and pride, God had to cast Lucifer and the angels who joined him in mutiny against God out of heaven. One third of the angels God created fell from heaven with Lucifer.

God is a pure and holy God. Heaven is a place of justice and righteousness. God has engineered the universe to function under righteous delegated authority. When Lucifer brought sin into heaven through pride and covetousness, God had to cast him from heaven or heaven would no longer be the place of perfect order God made it to be. In a moral and spiritual universe, sin must be judged.

God threw Lucifer and the fallen angels out of heaven into the heavenlies. Other angels were chained and cast into a vast place of great darkness called hell. God appointed them to deep, dark dungeons where they are still chained until the time of their judgment. Hell is a place of eternal punishment for beings that choose to be separated from God and His perfect plan. It is a place without escape for there is a great chasm that cannot be crossed. There is a lake made of fire and sulfur in hell and the fire cannot be put out. It is a place of darkness, weeping, torment and gnashing of teeth. Hell is everlasting separation from God.

Exiled from heaven Lucifer was consumed with anger and hate. His name was now changed to Satan. His objective is to destroy God's plan and the people He had created. A fierce passion to have mankind worship him instead of God burned as a consuming fire inside of him. This fallen angel knew how much God loved the man and woman He visited with every day. Satan desperately wanted to separate these people from God, just as he was. He wanted total control over the earth and mankind. He began formulating a plan to take God's creation, twist earth into a dark and corrupt place of rebellion against God.

The Fall of Man

From the heavenlies, where Satan and the fallen angels dwelled, he had access to both the third heaven and the earth. Satan observed as God, Adam, and Eve fellowshipped in the garden. He knew if he could get the man and the woman to eat from the tree of the knowledge of good and evil, mankind would die spiritually and be separated from God. He also knew God told Adam and Eve the fruit of this tree was forbidden to them. Satan planned a scheme to deceive them into eating the fruit God had forbidden. Once he tempted them into eating the fruit, sin or the knowledge of evil would infiltrate the human race and they would die spiritually.

One day Satan disguised as a serpent entered the Garden of Eden. He found Eve and boldly proclaimed to her that God was lying when He commanded them not to eat of this tree's fruit. His goal was to convince Adam and Eve God had an ulterior motive for not allowing them to eat the fruit of this spectacular tree. Satan's plan was to persuade them to rationalize what God had said, and doubt God's word. He approached the woman and said:

"Did God really say you must not eat the fruit from any of the trees in the garden?"

"Of course we may eat fruit from the trees in the garden," the woman replied "It's only the fruit from the tree in the middle

of the garden that we are not allowed to eat. God said, 'You must not eat it or even touch it; if you do, you will die.'"

"You won't die!" the serpent replied to the woman. "God knows that your eyes will be opened as soon as you eat it, and you will be like God, knowing both good and evil."

The woman was convinced. She saw that the tree was beautiful and its fruit looked delicious, and she wanted the wisdom it would give her. So she took some of the fruit and ate it. Then she gave some to her husband, who was with her, and he ate it, too. At that moment their eyes were opened, and they suddenly felt shame at their nakedness. So they sewed fig leaves together to cover themselves. (Genesis 3:1-7)

Lying has been Satan's craft right from the beginning. With this lie, he deceived Adam and Eve into clear disobedience of a specific Godly command. Sin now entered the human race. Satan tempted Eve to disobey God and His command that forbid a seemingly innocent action. By eating the fruit, Adam, as the representative of mankind, sought a source of wisdom apart from God in order to be morally independent of Him. They challenged the right of Almighty God to guide and direct their lives by exercising authority and power over their own lives. Adam and Eve declared their independence from God.

This one conversation between Satan and mankind changed the course of human history. Satan deceived the woman with a promise that she would be like God if she ate the forbidden fruit. By convincing the woman and consequently the man to be disobedient to God's Word, Satan was able to bring death and sin into the world. His diabolical plan was a success. If only Adam and Eve had believed God and understood the consequences of disobedience, the future of mankind would have been radically different.

The human race was created in the image of God, and therefore created sinless. If God forcibly prevented man from sinning, man would not have a free will. Without free choice, real love is impossible. It was decided from the beginning angels and mankind would have free will. All of God's created beings are given the freedom to believe what they choose to believe and to make their own individual choices.

Now mankind died spiritually and sin entered into all of the earth. This was the "fall of man", the separation of man from God. This was the second calamity Satan instigated. This event completely altered the original plan God intended for mankind. The forces of darkness were set free and the great spiritual war between good and evil was now on a new battleground called Earth.

It seemed that Satan had won.

When the cool evening breezes were blowing, the man and his wife heard the Lord God walking about in the garden. So they hid from the Lord God among the trees. Then the Lord God called to the man, "Where are you?" He replied, "I heard you walking in the garden, so I hid. I was afraid because I was naked."

"Who told you that you were naked?" the Lord God asked. "Have you eaten from the tree whose fruit I commanded you not to eat?"

The man replied, "It was the woman you gave me who gave me the fruit, and I ate it."

Then the Lord God asked the woman, "What have you done?"

"The serpent deceived me," she replied. "That's why I ate it." (Genesis 3:8-13)

The Creator established His covenant with Adam and Eve, but they did not keep the pact. God meant for them to be stewards over the earth He had created and entrusted to them. Man was to exercise dominion over creation and to be God's representatives. They were majestic beings created to rule over the earth and its creatures. God made them to tend and keep the garden and bring order and harmony to the physical earth. This first covenant concerned human sovereignty, responsibility and one moral prohibition. They were to refrain from eating the fruit of the tree of the knowledge of good and evil, under the penalty of death. Both the man and the woman blamed each other for what had happened but it was their own individual responsibility. They both chose to disobey God. The result of sin is death. After the fall of man, the human race and earth became a perversion of the majesty God had created.

> *Then the Lord God said, "Look, the human beings have become like us, knowing both good and evil. What if they reach out, take fruit from the tree of life, and eat it? Then they will live forever!" So the Lord God banished them from the Garden of Eden, and he sent Adam out to cultivate the ground from which he had been made. After sending them out, the Lord God stationed mighty cherubim to the east of the Garden of Eden. And he placed a flaming sword that flashed back and forth to guard the way to the tree of life. (Genesis 3:22-24)*

The sword of God's judgment stood between fallen man and God's garden. All during these events, the angels watched these things...

"When I look at the night sky and see the work of your fingers-
the moon and the stars you set in place- what are mere mortals
that you should think about them, human beings that you
should care for them? Yet you made them only a little lower
than God and crowned them with glory and honor.

(Psalm 8:3-5)

Chapter Two

INVISIBLE WARS

Angelic forces play a profound part in human lives and events.

When sin entered the human race, the forces of darkness were set free on earth and mankind was in a war, a spiritual war, where there are no physical, tangible enemies. Spiritual warfare exists in the unseen, supernatural dimension, where God is all-powerful and Satan is in revolt.

> *For we are not fighting against people made of flesh and blood, but against the evil rulers and authorities of the unseen world, against those mighty powers of darkness who rule this world, and against wicked spirits in the heavenly realms. (Ephesians 6:12)*

Satan the author of sin is the spiritual leader of wickedness in high places and the angels that rebelled against God now serve as demons. Together they became the principalities, powers, and rulers of the darkness over the planet earth and its inhabitants.

The relationship between God and man is not exclusive. There is a third party to contend with, the great opponent called Satan. He is incapable of fighting with God one against one, power against power, so he is determined to thwart God's plan. In his warfare against God Satan uses the human race. His all-consuming intent is to come between God and man; to cause a separation that cannot be reconciled.

There is a world of spirits, just beyond the human eye. A spiritual realm in another dimension which humans cannot see, yet each man and women's destiny is decided by whom they serve: God or Satan. Humans are spiritual creatures with free wills and must make a choice to live in light or darkness. Both angels and demons are involved in spiritual warfare that profoundly affects humans.

Angels Close Up

Angels possess knowledge people do not have and have a far greater power and might than men. They can only be in one place at one time, unlike God who is present in all places at the same time. While the holy angels have tremendous authority, they must choose to serve God. Like mankind, they must also face His righteous judgment.

Throughout history, there have been many stories of humans who have seen angels. Remember, angels do have the ability to make themselves visible. The accounts told of these angelic manifestations include descriptions of angels that appear to be so glorious and beautiful; they amaze and often frighten people who witness their presence. Some appear to have an aura of rainbow light around them so brilliant no human being can stand the brightness of them. Others appear like men dressed as humans or sometimes in pure bright linen, having their chests girded with golden bands. Their bodies may be colored to look like precious gems and their faces may look like lightning. Their eyes may appear like flaming torches, and their arms and legs like the gleam of a lustrous bronze. People have shared accounts where they were able to see awesome winged creatures visibly descending from heaven. Some have brilliance like the shining of the sun, illuminating the surroundings like flashes of lightning. Many angels manifest themselves to look just like a human, so you never know when you might be entertaining angels. It is always said to be a phenomenal encounter, proving there is an unseen supernatural world filled with angelic celestial beings.

Demons Close Up

Satan, mankind's archenemy, has divided the demons that follow him into organized ranks of authority and importance and He is the head of the powers of darkness and ignorance. It is like a military force that Satan fashioned after the model God used with His own angelic forces. Every person who lived on earth before this current millennial rule of Jesus had experienced the presence of Satan's evil power and that of the demons who served him. These evil spirits follow his devious bidding. They are dangerous and vicious, just as dedicated to their cause of destruction and death of humanity as Lucifer himself.

Demons have their own distinct personality; they think, speak, act, and have emotions. In the area of demon power, there are degrees and variations of abilities and governing by ruler spirits. Certain demons were assigned to exercise their influence over particular nations and individual cities. There was no true love or goodwill among demons; they are full of division, deep hatred and rivalry. There are various kinds of evil spirits including blind spirits, deaf spirits, deceiving spirits, seducing spirits, jealous spirits, familiar spirits, and insane spirits. Spirits of evil in the heavens caused great confusion on planet earth and to all of its inhabitants.

Many stories over the centuries came from people who believed they had seen demons. The descriptions given from those who had a glimpse of this part of the supernatural world were hideous. Demons were described as monstrous creatures, extremely repulsive to the eye and frightful to the heart. Some were very large and others quite small, but all looked physically abominable.

Angels and demons often engaged in warfare. Each human played a part in this gigantic struggle that affected the entire universe. God has so much love for the people He created, He appointed angels to guard over individual people as well as cities and nations, protecting them against these wicked beings.

Prior to this Millennium that we now live in, mankind was not only fighting against their own sinful natures and fleshly desires, but there was also a spiritual war going on all around them. The battle began in the mind of each individual, where Satan attacked them with thoughts meant to tempt them into sin, pervert their actions or harm themselves and others. Once man chose sin in the garden, all humans were subsequently born with a sinful nature and their minds were set on what their flesh desired. Man in his fallen state, being dead spiritually, did not want to submit to God's plan.

When you follow the desires of your sinful nature, your lives will produce these thoughts, eagerness for lustful pleasure, idolatry, participation in demonic activities, hostility, quarreling, jealousy, outbursts of anger, selfish ambition, divisions, the feeling that everyone is wrong except those in your own little group, envy, drunkenness, wild parties, and other kinds of sin. (Galatians 5:19-21)

All of these are the desires of the flesh, the temptations each person has to resist throughout their lives. These transgressions are against God; they are an act of self-will opposed to the will of God. Satan knew once sin entered the human race, each person has these thoughts and desires. Every person finds themselves in a battle against the sinful nature of their flesh. Satan wanted more than anything to tempt man into living a life filled with rebellion, because the result of sin was death and eternal separation from God.

Illegitimate Supernatural Power

Another tactic these rulers of darkness used against humans was the practice of supernatural phenomenon. Humans crave power and Satan had a certain amount of supernatural power to offer humans. Power that comes from demons is illegitimate power, yet people still loved experimenting with it, because it fulfills man's desire to control others and to know the unknown. These deceiving spirits claimed to answer profound questions about life. This illegitimate, supernatural power was demonstrated in many different ways including astrology, witchcraft, sorcery, magic, palm reading, fortune telling, mind altering drugs and other forms of mysticism. Necromancy or the conjuring of spirits from the dead was a disguised way of revealing future events or to influence them. The powers obtained by people, who participated in these forms and other types of occult practices, were demonically influenced. God prohibited humans from participating in the black arts. These demonic systems sought miracles outside of God. All supernatural activity outside of God's divine operation was from a demonic source. When man looked for information from Satan, they opened a "spiritual gate", allowing Satan and his demons to inflict their authority over and through these individuals.

Returning to the Garden of Eden, Eve also thought she was gaining a power through knowledge. However, she lost everything pertaining to true knowledge in God. She cried, "The serpent has deceived me"! God warned mankind about the deception of illegitimate principalities and powers. Humans that participated in these satanic activities were serving Satan. Like Adam and Eve, they were also deceived and opened a dangerous door to the unseen forces of darkness.

Demons desired human habitation. Their longing was for embodiment and they would take advantage of every opportunity they had to overtake or inhabit the spirit, mind and body of man or beast. They could not just possess someone; they had to be permitted access, one way or another. These demonic spirits entered people who practiced the occult, through continual sin, and through human evil choices. Once a demon spirit inhabited a human body, that person became what is called possessed. A possessed person was a puppet for the demon or demons that had inhabited their body. They would murder, rape, and commit all kinds of horrible crimes that were not of their own will. Some demonically possessed humans had supernatural physical strength provided by the demon or demons inside of them. Thousands of demons could live in one person at the same time. Demons had the ability to speak from the mouths of those who they possessed, most often with strange voices, saying whatever they wanted; mostly vile and evil things. Sometimes these manifestations caused physical sickness. Not all human diseases were demon-related, but some physical afflictions were caused by evil spirits.

Eternal Purposes

Satan patrolled the earth, "walking about like a roaring lion, seeking for someone to devour". He acquired many names including; *Abaddon, Appolyon, Beelzebub*, the *Devil, Power of Darkness*, and *Father of Lies*. Remember the first lie to humans was in the garden when he told Eve "you will not die". Satan was a tempter and corrupter of minds. He was also known as the *dragon*, the *serpent* and the *great deceiver* of the whole world. He became the "god of the world", the ruler of the power of the air, the spirit that worked in the children of disobedience.

Day and night Satan brought accusations against God's people. Man's great adversary knew if he was to prevent the purposes of God, he must attack the righteousness of God's chosen people.

God is omniscient or all-knowing. He is the beginning and the end, knowing everything that happens. He was not astounded when Lucifer rebelled and fell from heaven because of his pride. God was not startled when one third of His angels rebelled with Lucifer and were cast out from His presence. He knew Satan and his fallen angels would wage a war against mankind, and humans would not be able to stand defenseless against these principalities and powers.

God has a plan and a purpose for everything that happens. From the moment He created mankind there was a much higher intent for them than to be defeated by Satan, or for the whole world to be overcome with the darkness of sin. God never intended to leave mankind alone to fend for themselves against evil supernatural beings.

His master design serves a higher purpose in the overall plan of eternity. He created an eternally perfect people without disturbing free will. By permitting satanic temptation, mankind's faith and obedience to God were tested. The situations and circumstances in which Satan enticed man with were very severe. They learned through these temptations how to overcome the forces of evil. Satan was given power to afflict, but was kept in check. In all his evil work among humanity or in nature, he was still under God's authority and power.

God creates each human with a destiny and a purpose. Every person needs to develop particular strengths and God-given gifts so they can fulfill the eternal purposes God intended for them. Our Heavenly Father uses every situation in the lives of those who love Him and serve Him for eternal purpose. Just as statues are created from a hunk of rock and slowly chiseled away until the artistic piece emerges, God builds character in each person who loves Him, which is often developed by life's challenges.

Life is a training ground to prepare man for eternity. Mankind has to resist the temptations of their own sinful nature, and overcome the deception of Satan and the principalities and powers of darkness who serve him. God in his infinite wisdom, also used this predicament mankind was in to battle the powers of evil. God turned the fall of one third of his angelic creation, and the fall of man, into something worthy with eternal purpose.

And we know that God causes everything to work together for the good of those who love God and are called according to his purpose for them. (Romans 8:28)

At the conclusion of the last age, when Jesus returned to begin His Millennial Rule over Earth, an angel was sent down to earth with a special mission. Having the key to the bottomless pit and a great chain in his hand he took Satan and bound him up and cast him into the pit and set a seal on him so that he could not deceive the nations any more. Right now we do not have to fight these demonic powers like people had to in ages past, but after Jesus has ruled on Earth for one thousand years Satan must be loosed for a season.

How you are fallen from heaven, O shining star, son of the morning! You have been thrown down to the earth, you who destroyed the nations of the world. For you said to yourself, "I will ascend to heaven and set my throne above God's stars. I will preside on the mountain of the gods far away in the north. I will climb to the highest heavens and be like the Most High. But instead, you will be brought down to the place of the dead, down to its lowest depths.

(Isaiah 14: 12-15)

Chapter Three

A FRESH START

After Adam and Eve were expelled from the Garden of Eden and prohibited by angels from returning, mankind began to reproduce and their numbers greatly increased. As the years passed, there was a population explosion on earth.

People were consumed with sin and did not think it was worthwhile to embrace the knowledge of God. The human race was so filled with wickedness, every imagination and intention of human thinking was only evil.

"It is the thought-life that defiles you. For from within, out of a person's heart, come evil thoughts, sexual immorality, theft, murder, adultery, greed, wickedness, deceit, eagerness for lustful pleasure, envy, slander, pride, and foolishness. All these vile things come from within; they are what defile you and make you unacceptable to God." (Mark 7:20-23)

Because man had eaten from the tree of the knowledge of good and evil all humanity was corrupted with sin. Although they knew of God, they continued to do the very things opposed to God. Mankind rejected God and quickly because vicious and depraved. God observed their evil and violence.

Now the Lord observed the extent of the people's wickedness, and he saw that all their thoughts were consistently and totally evil. So the Lord was sorry he had ever made them. It broke his heart. (Genesis 6:5-6)

God was filled with sorrow, but He allowed sin to run its course as an act of judgement. God judges according to revealed truth, deeds, and the level of knowledge a person has. A holy, righteous God could not condone sin, nor can he tolerate it.

One Virtuous Man

There was a man named Noah who was a pleasure to God. He was the only truly virtuous man living on the earth among this evil generation. He taught the importance of obedience to God's righteous laws to the people around him. Noah was diligent to conduct his affairs according to God's will. He walked in fellowship with God.

So God said to Noah, "I have decided to destroy all living creatures, for the earth is filled with violence because of them. Yes, I will wipe them all from the face of the earth! (Genesis 6:13)

God revealed to Noah He would flood the earth with water. But God established a covenant with Noah. Noah his wife, his sons, and their wives, would be kept alive. God instructed Noah, in minute detail, the design of the ark he was to build. Noah was careful to thoroughly carry out each instruction God gave him.

When the ark was completed, representatives from every species of the animal kingdom were drawn to Noah. Two by two Noah brought every living creature found on land both male and a female they went into the boat with him to be kept alive and later repopulate the earth. Noah stored foods his family and animals would need. Noah did everything exactly as God commanded him.

When the people saw Noah building the ark, they scoffed at him, thinking he was crazy. There was no water anywhere that his ark could be launched. Responding to their ridicule, Noah told them of God's anger with their sin and tried to convince them they needed to turn from their wicked ways. He spoke to them of obedience and God's love, but they only laughed at Noah.

When the time was right, Noah led the creatures into the ark, two by two, both male and female, the footed, the crawling, and the winged creatures as God had commanded him.

Suddenly, the fountains within the earth burst open and spouted water. The wild rushing waters above the firmament broke through and poured down upon the earth. For forty days and nights water roared over the land and giant waves crashed upon the seas. The ark rose higher and higher until the flood covered the mountains and there was water everywhere over the earth. The ark gently floated upon the surface of the waters.

Every living creature on the land perished. Every creature with breath drowned. Below the ark, the drowning people entered a dreadful eternity apart from God. Only Noah and those who were with him survived.

After forty days the rain ceased. The fountains of the deep stopped and the windows of the heavens closed. Water continued to cover the earth for five months, but God remembered Noah and every living thing that was with him on the ark. He sent a strong wind across the earth and the waters began to recede.

In the seventh month the boat came to rest on the mountains of Ararat. The waters had subsided from the land and removing the covering of the ark he saw the ground was drying up. They had lived in the ark for one year and ten days.

God spoke to Noah saying;

"Leave the boat, all of you. Release all the animals and birds so they can breed and reproduce in great numbers." (Genesis 8:15-17)

Noah arose with his family, went out of the ark and built an altar to burn offerings to the Lord. When the Lord smelled the pleasant odor of the sacrifice He said,

"I will never again curse the earth, destroying all living things, even though people's thoughts and actions are bent toward evil from childhood. As long as the earth remains, there will be springtime and harvest, cold and heat, winter and summer, day and night." (Genesis 8:21-22)

This was one of the covenants God made with Noah, that He would never again destroy the earth with water. God also promised Noah and his children the fear of humans would be upon every beast of the land, every bird of the air, all that creeps upon the ground, and upon all the fish of the sea.

Then God said to Noah and his sons;

"I have placed my rainbow in the clouds. It is the sign of my permanent promise to you and to all the earth." (Genesis 9:13)

The beautiful rainbow God placed in the sky would always be a reminder of His mercy and compassion on all. Moreover, it is a sign of God's covenant, His binding agreement with all humanity to never destroy the earth with a flood.

Although this righteous man, Noah, and his family were saved, he and his offspring were descendants of Adam and carried in their hearts the inheritance of sin. God graciously made another covenant with man and promised never again to deal with sin by sending such a devastating deluge. God planned to deal with sin in a new and redemptive way.

Stairway to Heaven

Mankind again multiplied in great numbers and soon the land was thickly populated. At this point in history, the whole world had only one language. Family after family they spread eastward until they found a pleasant plain in Shinar where they settled. The people who lived there began to talk about building a great city, with a temple-tower reaching to the skies, an eternal monument to themselves. It would bind them together and keep them from being scattered all over the world. The people's plans were egotistical, proud and a declaration of their rebellious desire to be independent of God. They undertook a united and godless effort to establish for themselves a figurative stairway to heaven. They made bricks by baking mud and mortared them with tar. The people went to work, building a monument from the ground up into the sky.

Then the Lord God came down to see the city and the tower that the men were building and He said,

"Look!" he said. "If they can accomplish this when they have just begun to take advantage of their common language and political unity, just think of what they will do later. Nothing will be impossible for them! Come let's go down and give them different languages. Then they won't be able to understand each other." (Genesis 11:6-7)

If the whole human race remained united in the proud attempt to take its destiny into its own hands by its man-centered efforts, there would be no limit to their unrestrained rebellion against God. Humankind would become as evil and wicked as they were before the Flood.

The name of that tower was Babel, because it was there the Lord confused the languages of the people so they would not understand each other. They ceased working together, building or living together. Like dust, the people were scattered across the face of the whole earth. Were it not for human arrogance, this division would not have been necessary.

At this point in history there had been three great judgments on sinful humanity. The first was the expulsion from Eden, the second was the Flood and the third was the scattering of the people from Babel. Because God is righteous, His judgments were necessary but God had not given up on this creation of His called man. His great plan to redeem them was still to unfold.

For the Lord is high above the nations; his glory is far greater than the heavens. Who can be compared with the Lord our God, who is enthroned on high? Far below him are the heavens and the earth. He stoops to look.

(Psalm 113:4-6)

Part Two

THE MASTER PLAN

Chapter Four

THE CHOSEN ONES

❧

God's plan of salvation for the human race was to be introduced through a nation and culture unlike any that had preceded it. He was to establish His rule on earth, for without God's restraint and influence, man would be totally depraved. He sought a man who was righteous in his heart; someone would trust in His word and be obedient to Him. He needed a person who had extraordinary faith and longed to have a relationship with God. This man would be the beginning of an exclusive group of people, chosen by God to be the ones He would use to communicate His message of love and deliverance.

This was the beginning of another covenant between God and mankind that would benefit humanity. Not only did God choose a particular people to do His works through, He created a specific nation and city for His people to function from. From one end of the universe to the other, such a great concept as this was never heard of before. God was taking a nation for Himself from the midst of other nations. God was establishing this nation so His great plan for mankind would unfold at the perfect time.

I have a plan for the whole earth, for my mighty power reaches throughout the world. The Lord Almighty has spoken- who can change his plans? When his hand moves, who can stop him?" (Isaiah 14: 26-27)

God chose a man named Abraham to be the father of these special elect of people. Abraham was a man of great faith and listened when God spoke to him and obeyed His commands. God told him to leave his own country and people and to occupy the land He would guide him to possess. Abraham did as God commanded him. He, his wife and servants took all of their possessions and traveled to this "Promised Land". God brought him to a beautiful countryside with fertile plains and a river that watered the region.

God made a covenant with Abraham giving him and all of his descendants this God-ordained land. He clearly defined the boundaries to Abraham, from the river of Egypt to the river Euphrates. The western boundary of the Promised Land was the Mediterranean coast and the eastern border which included the highland plateau beyond the Jordan River in the territory of Bashan. He gave this land to Abraham and to all of his descendants forever. He told Abraham to establish his family there; this land "flowing with milk and honey". He not only gave Abraham the promise of land, but He told Abraham his descendants would become a great nation. As long as this chosen people diligently obeyed the voice of God, the Lord would set them high above all nations of the earth. They were obligated by this condition of the covenant established by God & Abraham.

> *For you are a holy people, who belong to the Lord your God.*
> *Of all the people on earth, the Lord your God has chosen you*
> *to be his own special treasure. (Deuteronomy 7: 6)*

God also promised Abraham he would accomplish great things and his name would be celebrated. His life would be marked by God's personal blessings and would be the channel of God's blessing to many people around him. God promised He would start a spiritual movement through him that would influence every nation of the earth, and all the families of the earth would be blessed. Part of God's covenant with Abraham would affect him personally and part of the covenant reached far beyond him to benefit humanity in general.

Substitute Payment

Another covenant God later established with the Hebrew nation (which was later called Israel) was the blood sacrifice. An animal sacrifice was brought to the priest who would lay his hands upon the animal, transferring the sins of the people to the animal. It was a system where God accepted a substitution blood payment for man's sin. Man needed to constantly be reminded the human race had sinned and died. They needed redemption from sin and the only payment accepted by God was the blood sacrifice.

By following these laws the chosen people showed reverent fear of the Creator by being obedient. Because they were obedient, God was able to cover them with all of the blessings of heaven. Obedience to God is always the key to blessings being manifested. Success as individuals and as a nation depended on the degree of their conformity to God's moral, civil and ceremonial laws.

These chosen people had the task of gaining control of this chosen land from the tribes who were living there. This did not happen easily and many battles ensued as they fought to keep this Promised Land for themselves. God revealed Himself to them in several ways; by trials, signs, wonders, victories and great terrors. He spoke to specific individuals Himself, and enabled others to prove of His existence through acts of supernatural phenomenon. Angels were also sent to convey messages concerning God's plans, and sometimes gave individuals supernatural guidance and direction.

Abraham and his family prospered much there and accumulated great wealth. Abraham's descendants grew into a mighty nation and great in number. God had a nation he would touch all tribes of the earth through. He had a people He could use to send His message of love for mankind. Through this chosen people He would gather a vast multitude to Himself out of every tribe, tongue, and nation.

And do not forget the things I have done throughout history. For I am God- I alone! I am God, and there is no one else like me. Only I can tell you what is going to happen even before it happens. Everything I plan will come to pass, for I do whatever I wish. (Isaiah 46: 9 – 10)

All of the Hebrew children were taught the history of this nation, the laws and the customs God had established with them. They reverentially passed this on from generation to generation. Stories of the awesome ways God intervened on Israel's behalf against many enemies were kept sacred and diligently written down, as well as the covenant God established with His people. Each generation learned to have great faith in the true Living God, knowing He was intimately involved in the prosperity and protection of their nation, Israel. God had chosen these people to be made into a holy nation of priests for God, his treasured possession.

O Lord my God, how great you are! You are robed with honor and with majesty; you are dressed in a robe of light. You stretch out the starry curtain of the heavens, you lay out the rafters of your home in the rain clouds. You make the clouds your chariots; you ride upon the wings of the wind.

(Psalm 104: 1-3)

Chapter Five

THE LAW

❦

G od knew that humans need laws to govern themselves with, so we can distinguish right from wrong. Mankind needs a foundation of truth in order to live righteously. These truths enable us to resist and understand the sin that infiltrated the human race. God's laws are an important weapon He has provided for our battle against sin. If man chooses to obey these laws, exposure to the darkness of sin is limited and we do not have to endure the consequences of sin. Success as individuals and as a nation depends on the degree of our conformity to God's law.

God sent His laws to humanity through the nation of Israel and communicated them through men whose hearts were His, through miracles, and natural phenomenon. Some of these men who brought His laws to mankind were willing to obey God even though they would be laughed at, persecuted, and martyred. Most people want God to change the laws of the universe to what they desire! He predetermined laws and divine authority through which the universe operates. His plans do not change; God is the same yesterday, today, and forever throughout the ages.

Top of the Mountain

There was a man named Moses whom God had selected to lead the Hebrews. On the appointed day, God called Moses to the top of the mountain and he gave him the first part of his new system of laws for his people - the Ten Commandments.

There are ten moral laws, the first four are statutes to God and the other six are statutes to others.

1. Do not worship any other god than the one true God. All other gods are false gods.

2. Do not make idols or images in the form of God. An idol can be anything (or anyone) you worship by giving it more importance than God. If something (or someone) has your time, attention and affections, it has your worship. It could be an idol in your life.

3. Do not treat God's name lightly or with disrespect. Because of God's importance, his name is always to be spoken of with honor.

4. Dedicate or set aside a regular day each week for Sabbath rest and worship of the Lord.

5. Give honor to your father and mother by treating them with respect and obedience.

6. Do not deliberately kill a fellow human being.

7. Do not have sexual relations with anyone other than your spouse. God forbids sex outside of the bounds of marriage.

8. Do not steal or take anything that doesn't belong to you..

9. Do not tell a lie about someone or bring a false accusation against another person.

10. Do not desire anything or anyone that does not belong to you. Comparing yourself to others and longing to have what they have leads to jealousy, envy and other sins. Be content by focusing on the blessings God has given you and not what he has not given you.

God's Mirror

God wrote these laws with His own finger and placed them on tablets made of rock. He commanded the Hebrews to build a special place to keep these commandments called the Ark of the Covenant. They would always have them close by, to teach their children and pass them along from generation to generation. They serve as a constant reminder of the covenant between mankind and God.

God also established laws for eating, personal hygiene, and government. He taught His statutes on marriage and children to guide successful functioning families. He gave laws against participating in occult practices such as sorcery, witchcraft, and fortune telling of future events. The more He taught mankind to function within the laws of His universe the closer man would be to the original purpose and destiny God intended. These laws give mankind direct instructions regarding the actions and thoughts that God does or does not approve of.

God's law is a reflection of His holy character and His purposes for mankind. His law guides and helps us in developing our character. They are the minimum standard of conduct that God requires and the basis for judgment for those who disobey. These laws were never meant to be a system of words to gain approval or spiritual merit. They uncover the dark side of human nature and define such behavior as morally wrong. The law points to our need for grace and mercy.

The law applies to those to whom it was given, for its purpose is to keep people from having excuses and to bring the entire world into judgment before God. For no one can ever be made right in God's sight by doing what his law commands. For the more we know God's law, the clearer it becomes that we aren't obeying it. (Romans 3: 19 – 20)

God's law is like a mirror. Mirrors are helpful, because they reveal truth to us.

He sends his orders to the world- how swiftly his word flies!
He sends the snow like white wool; he scatters frost upon the
ground like ashes. He hurls the hail like stones. Who can stand
against his freezing cold? Then, at his command, it all melts.
He sends his winds, and the ice thaws.

(Psalm 147: 15 –18)

Chapter Six

MESSENGERS

G od so loved the world He wanted His plans to be revealed to humanity. He particularly wanted His children to understand His actions. In order to reveal His plans, He selected a chosen people who established the nation of Israel. Out of these chosen people God called forth prophets, whose assignment was to speak God's Word to the world. They were God's mouthpieces or messengers. The Holy Spirit was sent to these prophets and supernaturally enabled them to speak of future events. This is one way God permitted certain people to have legitimate access to the world of supernatural power.

God revealed Himself to prophets in visions and spoke to them in dreams. Often He sent angels to them with messages from heaven. God spoke directly to the consciousness of the prophets. When the Spirit of God would rest upon these chosen ones they were supernaturally enabled to speak about the future. Once this power came over them, they would begin prophesying out loud, making bold claims on specific issues God had told them to speak about. The prophecies these men and women spoke established their credentials as Spirit-empowered leaders. Prophecy never had its origin in the will of man, but men spoke from God as they were prompted by the Holy Spirit.

During the time Israel had kings, they employed many prophets because they understood they were being used by God to speak to them. Those kings who listened and acted upon these genuine messages God was providing through these prophets, prospered greatly and were victorious in battles against their enemies. For some of the military leaders and kings, God would reveal how their enemies would attack and what the counter strategy should be. There were many times when the odds were against the armies of Israel, they were so outnumbered that it seemed there was no hope. Supernaturally through prophets, God revealed to them how to overcome the circumstances. The Israelites learned when they listened to the words from God through the prophets, and lived in obedience to His laws, they experienced great victories.

"But always, first of all, I warn you through my servants the prophets. I, the Sovereign Lord, have now done this." (Amos 3:7)

Many of the prophecies contained information about powerful empires that would later rule on earth. Other prophecies concerned the future of Israel, both the victories and failures she would go through.

Proclamations of a Savior

There were prophecies being proclaimed to the elect for thousands of years concerning a Messiah, the Savior of the world. God told the Israelites He was sending His own Son. In great detail prophets spoke of this Messiah who would be born of a virgin in a place called Bethlehem. Prophecies proclaimed that a brilliant star would announce His birth and He would be a prophet Himself, and also a Priest, Judge and a King. The Messiah would be the ruler of Israel and a direct descendent of Abraham. He would be called Wonderful Counselor, and the King who would introduce His royal Kingdom causing the whole world to marvel. Prophets called this promised Savior the Prince of Peace. His rule would bring wholeness and well being to individuals, nations and societies. It was written He would have divine power, as well as an everlasting compassion for people, as healer, provider and protector. This Messiah would be anointed by the Holy Spirit and have great zeal for God. His ministry would take place in the area of Galilee. These prophecies proclaimed the Messiah's ministry would include great miracles and He would be a teacher of parables. The Christ would be a Jew and would enter Jerusalem on a donkey, prior to His crucifiction. For centuries, the Jewish people anxiously awaited this promised Savior who had been revealed to them through numerous specific, detailed prophecies.

The prophets also spoke of this Messiah having great sorrows involved in His visit to earth. He would be despised, rejected and forsaken by men. The prophets said this Christ would be betrayed by a friend for silver and would be accused by false witnesses yet remain silent before His accusers. He would be scourged and wounded, smitten and spit upon, mocked and the object of scorn. The Messiah's hands and feet were to be pierced and He would be put to death alongside transgressors. He would suffer great thirst and be given vinegar to drink. When He died, darkness would cover the land until three o'clock and He would be buried in a rich man's tomb. The prophets told of these future events concerning this Messiah with profound detail.

One of the greatest prophecies told concerning this Messiah was about His death and resurrection. Three days after He died, He would rise from the dead and ascend to heaven and be seated at the right hand of God. His ever expanding, peaceful government would never end and He would rule all of the nations of the world with perfect fairness and justice. He would take up man's infirmities and carry their sorrows.

But he was wounded and crushed for our sins. He was beaten that we might have peace. He was whipped, and we were healed! (Isaiah 53:5)

His life would be offered for restitution of God's righteous judgment concerning mankind's sins. In the past God provided the substitute of the blood sacrifice of an animal as the atonement or payment for man's sin, but the Messiah would be the final perfect sacrifice that paid the price for all sin. The prophets told Israel this would happen, because the Lord had established this great plan of salvation for all of mankind.

Divine Guidance

Eventual fulfillment is the test of true prophecy. If a prophet spoke of an event that did come to pass, he earned the reverence due to him from the people. If the prophet's words were found reliable and accurate, everyone knew and believed God. This omnipotent power from another dimension called heaven was truly speaking to them and giving them divine guidance. What human had the capability to predict the future and make great armies fall? Prophecy was a powerful testimony of God's existence and His desire to reveal His plans. It was also a testimony God's covenant with His people was real and He really did love them. Prophecy established trust in God.

God's methods are puzzling to humans, because we are not omniscient like Him. If the prophetic message was for the distant future, the prophet's words did not make sense to the generation hearing them. It was often disclosed to these prophets the services they were rendering were not meant for themselves or their time period, but for people who would be alive in future generations. God's prophets provided these messages about the future so, even future generations would read them and understand the power, glory, and reality of God's plan.

> *They were told that these things would not happen during their lifetime, but many years later, during yours. And now this Good News has been announced by those who preached to you in the power of the Holy Spirit sent from heaven. It is all so wonderful that even the angels are eagerly watching these things happen. (I Peter 1:12)*

As God provided prophecies about the future, He also warned about false prophets who would only use intelligent foresight masquerading as prophecy. He admonished us to be aware of others whose prophecies would be based on coincidental fulfillment. These false prophets claimed to have received revelations from God, when in reality, their messages only proclaimed what their hearers wanted to hear. Many fall into the cunning trap of false prophecy.

Understanding the reality that God is revealing the grand plan and purposes He has established for all of creation through prophecy is perhaps the greatest testimony of the fact that the Bible was written for us by the Creator of the universe. Critical historical events, specific dispensations of time, God's plans and purposes are all revealed through biblical prophecy.

Forever, O Lord, your word stands firm in heaven. Your faithfulness extends to every generation, as enduring as the earth you created. Your laws remain true today, for everything serves your plans.

(Psalm 119: 89-91)

Chapter Seven

SPIRITUAL BATTLES

❧❦❧

The Jews were a very prosperous people with a land of fertile rich soil, numerous livestock and a sense of security knowing the God who created the universe was interested in their welfare. They continued to multiply in numbers and grew into a flourishing nation. They had been chosen to be the people God would work His great plan for humanity through.

This was what God had promised Abraham, he would make him into a great nation and bless all others through him. His descendants would be numerous as the stars of heaven, or the sands of the seashore. This land would be an everlasting possession to Abraham's descendants. These promises were conditional and depended upon their keeping the commands of God, thereby keeping their covenant with God. Obedience is necessary to walk in God's blessings.

Not only had God provided them with a nation of their own, He gave them the city of Jerusalem. The Jewish people built a special temple within this city to honor their God, a place where God would abide among them. This was the designated place where they made sacrifices to Him in order to renew their covenant, one with the other. They kept the Ark of the Covenant in the temple. In the very center of the temple was a place called the Most Holy Place where the appointed priests would experience the glory and presence of God.

Created for Worship

The people who lived outside the nation of Israel were also great in number. Some tribes built cities, some farmed, and others lived in tents and wandered through the vast wilderness with flocks and herds. In each individual culture, they acquired skills of music, painting, theater and various forms of art. They developed many different alphabets from which languages were derived. There were many cultures surrounding the tribes of Israel.

From many other kingdoms came people who had false gods of their own. Some of these nations had thousands of gods or deities they worshipped. There were gods for every aspect of life including fertility, the sky and the sun. They had gods for prosperity and for the weather. Some of them worshipped animals, while others built idols of wood or metal, and prayed to them for help and guidance. Still others worshipped themselves and believed they were gods.

However, all mankind is aware somewhere deep in the very depths of their souls there is a higher power beyond creation. God made it plain since the creation of the world His invisible qualities, His eternal power and His divine nature. Humans always reach out to intangible sources of power. We have a common need and a desire to have a relationship with a God. We are created for worship. If we do not worship the true and living God by the power of the Holy Spirit, then we resort to one of the many counterfeits. We accept other forms of religion and sometimes unknowingly worship Satan.

All humans are made up of three parts the body, spirit, and soul. The body serves as a place to live in while we are on the earth, but because of the fall of man in the garden, the body must grow old and die. The soul of each man is made up of his mind, emotions, and will. The spirit is that eternal part of man that instinctively discerns the presence of this higher power, a God. It is here that the human race is connected to God because God is spirit. When the human body dies, the spirit that lived in that body goes on to another dimension, it does not die. Human spirits are created to live eternally.

Slipping Into Sin

God had instructed the people of Israel not to mingle with the people outside of the nation of Israel. He knew their false gods and sins would have a negative influence on His people. Unfortunately, the Israelites were like many prior generations; they did not want to be told what to do so many lived in rebellion to God's instructions.

Do not intermarry with them, and don't let your daughters and sons marry their sons and daughters. They will lead your young people away from me to worship other gods. Then the anger of the lord will burn against you, and he will destroy you. (Deuteronomy 7: 3-4)

So little by little, through marriages with gentile nations or non-Jewish nations, the chosen people intermingled with pagan cultures. The temptations to eat foods they were told by God they should not eat were overwhelming. Some of their ungodly sexual practices were enticing to them. Could something feeling so good be against God's laws? What harm could come from this wooden statue? They questioned God's laws and authority in their lives. The mothers and fathers of these Gentile nations saw no harm in giving their children idols to play with or worship, so why not allow our children? Soon, the next generation was worshipping false gods. As time went by, the memories of the mighty signs and wonders their forefathers saw, the prophecies spoken and the stories of Abraham and God's laws began to fade from their collective memory. By degrees Israel slipped into sin.

Satan and his demonic forces were at work. Spiritual warfare was their method of operation. The powers from the dark side knew if they could tempt these chosen people of God

with sin and rebellion, they could break through this covenant God established with Israel. Demonic forces knew by
enticing humans to sin they could disturb the power of God's
blessings over the Jewish people. Satan understands the
appetites of man's nature and how easily they are enticed to
sin. The choices they were making now were made according
to their own desires instead of God's laws.

God did not ask the Jews to stay away from Gentiles because He did not want them to enjoy themselves. God did not
give them the laws to live by because He thought life should
not be fun. God established these laws because He created the
universe to function in an orderly manner. He knew mingling
with other ungodly nations would lead to separation from
Him because it would lead them to sin. He designed His
creation to function under the laws of righteousness, justice
and holiness. When humans function under His laws they
flow with His universal laws. When the Israelites followed
God's wise guidance they would not be under a curse.

As God's chosen people turned away from Him and did
as they pleased sin began to take its toll. The anger of the
Lord was kindled against them and God allowed enemies to
rise up against His chosen people.

The pattern of their behavior was a vicious cycle. Over
and over again the generations that had known and obeyed
the Lord passed away and the next one would forget the
glory that belonged to Israel when they were obedient to

Him. Inevitably, Israel would suffer at the hand of a new enemy, because they were no longer functioning under the umbrella of God's blessing and protection. They were driven into slavery and removed from the land God had given them until many generations later.

The history of man is filled with stories of thousands of wars that were fought in order to gain power and land by taking control over other kingdoms. When they were suffering from oppression from the many enemies that surrounded them, Israel remembered the Lord their God and how He had been there in the past for their ancestors who would cry to Him for deliverance. Marvelous is the mercy of the Lord! He always brought His people back to peace and rest again. Again and again, the Lord God would send a deliverer to His people. Deliverance and redemption was God's gift to Israel even though they were rebellious and suffered much for their disobedience.

No, God has not rejected his own people, whom he chose from the very beginning. Do you remember what the Scriptures say about this? Elijah the prophet complained to God about the people of Israel and said, "Lord, they have killed your prophets and torn down your altars. I alone am left, and now they are trying to kill me, too." And do you remember God's reply? He said, "You are not the only one left. I have seven thousand others who have never bowed down to Baal!" (Romans 11: 2 – 4)

There was always a remnant though, a group of obedient people who remembered the covenant God had with Israel. The laws and promises God established with Israel were never totally beyond recollection. He has always worked with a faithful minority who loved Him enough to stand against the tide of the wicked world systems. Out of this "remnant" His promise to Abraham was fulfilled. The entire world would be blessed because of Abraham, just as God promised. God told His people righteousness would eventually triumph. Utopia would eventually come to earth and the Kingdom of God would ultimately prevail. He continued to send messages through His prophets about a Savior. One who would come to earth and reconcile mankind to God.

What could possibly save mankind from the unseen power that controlled this dark world and the spiritual hosts of evil arrayed against them in heavenly warfare? Was there anything that could save humans from their own evil desires and the sin nature they struggled against? What could God do to stop the vicious cycle of rebellion Israel found herself in? The angels watched as planet earth and mankind raced towards their meeting with destiny...

Praise the Lord with melodies on the lyre; make music for him on the ten- stringed harp. Sing new songs of praise to him; play skillfully on the harp and sing with joy. For the word of the Lord holds true, and everything he does is worthy of our trust. He loves whatever is just and good, and his unfailing love fills the earth.

(Psalm 33:2-5)

Part Three

PROMISES KEPT

Chapter Eight

THE MORNING STAR

❧

As time passed, Israel ceased to be an independent nation and became a minor territory in a succession of larger empires. Control over this country was continually changing depending on what kingdom dominated that part of the world. First, the powerful Babylonian empire acquired Israel, followed by the Medo-Persians ruling. The Greeks overtook the area from Persia and finally an expanding Roman empire ruled over many nations including Israel.

During these unhappy years of oppression and internal strife, the Jewish people produced a large amount of literature. There were many Jews living outside of the nation of Israel who spoke different languages and lived in various cultures. However, they retained their national culture and religious identity. Their words, stories, and laws were recorded over the centuries and translated into other languages so everything that God had revealed to them would not be forgotten. The laws and prophecies given to mankind through this chosen nation and people were still being passed down generation to generation. There was always a remnant of committed, faithful people among the Jews.

Messages from Gabriel

As the generations passed these chosen people continued to wait for a Savior, the one that the prophets had spoken about for so long. When the time was right God sent a remarkable sign to a priest named Zechariah. The angel named Gabriel, appeared to him and told him his wife she would bear a son and he was to name him John. The angel explained this child would be great in the sight of the Lord and would be filled with the Holy Spirit even from birth. Gabriel also said this child would bring back many of the Jewish people to their God and John would prepare the people for the Messiah's entrance into the world. Zechariah knew his son had a special assignment in the coming events God was initiating. This child was a miracle because Zechariah and his wife Elizabeth were well along in years and she was barren.

The angel's words came to pass and Zechariah and his wife were blessed with a son they named John as God commanded them. Zechariah was filled with the Holy Spirit and prophesied; "This son will be called a prophet of the Most High and he will go before the Lord to prepare the way for Him". The Holy Spirit had supernaturally enabled

Zechariah to see into the future and predict his son's life and what he would accomplish for God.

Six months later Gabriel was sent to Nazareth and he appeared to a righteous virgin named Mary. Gabriel told Mary God highly favored her and she would soon be with child and give birth to a son. This baby would be the Son of God. Mary asked the angel how this could be because she was a virgin. Gabriel answered,

> "The Holy Spirit will come upon you, and the power of the Most High will overshadow you. So the baby born to you will be holy, and he will be called the Son of God." (Luke 1:35)

When this happened to Mary, she was already engaged to a man named Joseph. Before they came together, she was found to be pregnant through the power of the Holy Spirit. When Joseph heard Mary was pregnant and knew they had not been together as husband and wife, he assumed she had been with another man. An angel of the Lord appeared to him in a dream saying,

> "Do not be afraid to go ahead with your marriage to Mary. For the child within her has been conceived by the Holy Spirit. (Matthew 1:20)

Joseph did as the angel of the Lord commanded him and took Mary as his wife.

Good News of Great Joy

Joseph was a direct descendent of Abraham. This was a fulfillment of another ancient prophecy; all nations would be blessed through Abraham. A prophecy written hundreds of years earlier also came to pass; a virgin would give birth to a son.

All right then, the Lord himself will choose the sign. Look! The virgin will conceive a child! She will give birth to a son and will call him Immanuel- God is with us. (Isaiah 7:14)

As the time drew close for His birth the Roman governor issued a decree a census should be taken. Every Jew was to return to their home to register. Mary and Joseph headed to Bethlehem because his ancestors were from there. When they arrived in Bethlehem the time came for the baby to be born. Mary gave birth to her firstborn. This fulfilled another prophecy; "From Bethlehem, one will go before me to be ruler in Israel." The prophets had declared the Messiah would come from Bethlehem and God arranged for Mary and Joseph to be there when the child was born.

An angel appeared to some shepherds who were living out in the fields nearby. The glory of the Lord shone around them, and the shepherds were terrified. But the angel said to them,

"Don't be afraid!" he said. "I bring you good news of great joy for everyone! The Savior- yes, the Messiah, the Lord- has been

born tonight in Bethlehem, the city of David! And this is how you will recognize him: you will find a baby lying in a manger, wrapped snugly in strips of cloth!" (Luke2: 10-14)

The shepherds went to Bethlehem to see this wonderful child who was the promised Messiah. They found the baby and worshipped Him and told everyone they could what the angel had said concerning this child.

Meanwhile to the east of Jerusalem, a group of wise men called Magi had been following a great star in the sky. Having knowledge of the Jewish prophecies they knew this star signified the birth of the King, they also wanted to worship Him. These wise men came before Herod the governor of the land and asked where this child was. When the governor heard their story he was very disturbed. He called together the chief priests and teachers of the Jewish law, and inquired where the Messiah of the prophecies was to be born, under the guise he wanted to worship the Messiah. They told him in Bethlehem.

Herod knew the prophecies concerning this child who was the long awaited Savior the Jewish people had been longing for. According to prophecy, Christ or the Messiah was to be given total authority and power over the chosen people of Israel. Herod was very intimidated by this possibility and determined to be the only ruler over the Jews. Already the Messiah had an enemy.

The Magi followed the star in the sky until it illuminated the place where the Child lay in Bethlehem. When they found the Christ Child they worshipped Him and gave Him valuable gifts of gold, frankincense and myrrh. Then, they were warned in a dream not to return to Herod, but to leave by another route. Another prophecy had come true which said; a star would announce the birth of the Messiah.

Prepare the Road For the Lord

On the eighth day of His life he was circumcised according to Judaic law and He was named Jesus. When Joseph and Mary had done everything required by the law they returned to Galilee to their own town of Nazareth. When Jesus was twelve years old, He was found in the temple courts sitting among the teachers, listening to them and asking them questions. All who heard this young Man were astonished and overwhelmed with bewilderment and wonder at His intelligence, understanding and wisdom. At this young age, He was already recognized as a great Teacher. Jesus grew in wisdom, stature and had favor with God and men.

His cousin, John, grew up and became strong in spirit. He lived in the desert eating honey and locusts, dressed in clothes made of camel hair. John's simple food, clothing and lifestyle were a visual protest against self-indulgence. The time came for John, known as the Prophet and the Baptist to begin preaching in the desert. He announced to the chosen people they must repent or reconsider their choices; to regret their sins and change their conduct. He announced the Kingdom of heaven was at hand. People came from all around the country to hear John and confessed their sins. He taught water baptism would signify repentance for their sins. Those who chose to do this were submerged in the water of the Jordan River.

Every Jew who sought John reasoned and questioned in their hearts if John might possibly be the long awaited Christ. John told them he baptized them with water, but he was not the Messiah. The One coming was to baptize them with the Holy Spirit and with fire. This was also written in the book of a prophet,

> Listen! I hear the voice of someone shouting, "Make a highway for the Lord through the wilderness. Make a straight smooth road through the desert for our God. (Isaiah 40:3)

Even John's life was the fulfillment of yet another prophecy written long before he was born.

Then Jesus came to the Jordan to be baptized by John. When John saw Jesus he said,

> "Look! There is the Lamb of God who takes away the sin of the world! (John 1:29)

As a prophet, John immediately knew Jesus was the promised Savior. At the moment Jesus was baptized, He came up out of the water and heaven was opened. The Spirit of God descended like a dove and landed on Him. A voice from heaven said,

> *"This is my beloved Son, and I am fully please with him."*
> *Matthew (3:17)*

This was a fulfillment of the prophet's words that declared; "the Spirit of the Lord would rest upon Him, the Spirit of wisdom and understanding, the Spirit of counsel and strength, the Spirit of knowledge and the fear of the Lord".

The Great Temptation

Jesus was thirty years old when all of this happened. It was time He began His public ministry. Shortly after this Jesus was led into the desert and was fasting for forty days and nights. Then the tempter came to Him and said;

> *"If you are the Son of God, change these stones into loaves of*
> *bread." (Matthew 4:3)*

Satan is very articulate and uses speech to deceive people. He knows the best time to tempt us so knowing Jesus had not eaten, he tempted His flesh with food. Despite His hunger,

Jesus recognized that Satan was trying to deceive Him and replied,

> "No! The Scriptures say, 'People need more than bread for their life; they must feed on every word of God.' (Matthew 4:4)

When this appeal to the flesh failed, the Devil next appealed to the pride of life. Satan led Jesus to a very high mountain and showed Him in an instant all the kingdoms of the world and their splendor.

> The Devil told him, "I will give you the glory of these kingdoms and authority over them- because they are mine to give to anyone I please. I will give it all to you if you will bow down and worship me." (Luke 4:6-7)

Jesus answered,

> "The Scriptures say, "You must worship the Lord your God; serve only him." (Luke 4:8)

Next, the devil led Jesus to Jerusalem and had Him stand on the highest point of the temple and said;

> "If You are the Son of God, jump off! For the Scriptures say, He orders his angels to protect and guard you. And they will hold you with their hands to keep you from striking your foot on a stone." (Luke 4:9-11)

Jesus responded,

"The Scriptures also say, 'Do not test the Lord your God.' (Luke :12)

The devil gave his best shot at tempting and deceiving Jesus, but he could not succeed against the Son of Man! The two greatest challenges the devil ever had were the temptation of Adam and Eve and the temptation of Jesus. In both cases the results would be great for the devil, having far reaching consequences. The result of Eve's sinning was great and gained a definite victory for Satan. However he failed to tempt Jesus and this failure had many spiritual consequences that affected all men.

It is very interesting Satan quoted God's written words to Jesus, though he misused them. Satan kept in touch with all God had taught mankind through the Jews and had deviously memorized the words God had given them to write down. Even more fascinating is that Jesus fought off Satan's temptations with God's written words. The word of God or the Bible is one of the most effective weapons God provided humans with for victory in our battle with the devil and Jesus demonstrated this perfectly!

Angels came and ministered to Jesus and then He returned from the desert filled with the power of the Holy Spirit.

Good News

Many times Jesus spoke directly to the leaders of the Jews, telling them they were hypocrites and did not live what they preached. He accused them of being more concerned about keeping their ceremonies than about being moral. The Jewish religious leaders were adding rules and regulations to the authentic law of the Jews. Doing nothing to help others obey the law in faith, they instead invented ways to circumvent the laws of God by enforcing man-made rules and regulations.

Outwardly, these religious Jews appeared to honor the prophets in building or rebuilding memorials, but inwardly they rejected God and the Christ the prophets announced. They lived in opposition to the teachings of the prophets, just as many of their forefathers had done. Jesus made many enemies among His own people, because He confronted them with truth. The Jewish leaders were determined to trap Jesus and be rid of Him.

Jesus went throughout the area teaching and preaching the good news of the Kingdom of God, or God's way of doing things. The people were amazed at His teachings because He taught them as one who had authority, not as the other teachers of the law.

Jesus taught there was a place called heaven and a place called hell. The kingdom of Heaven was described as a

beautiful place where there would be no more death, suffering or tears; a virtual paradise. Conversely, hell was a place of
eternal sorrow, torment; gnashing of teeth and separation
from God. The choices of a human's life on earth would
determine where they would spend eternity, in heaven or
hell. He taught they needed to enter the Kingdom of God
through the narrow gate, as the gate to destruction was
broad. The gate to life was narrow and only a few find it.

> *Their judgment is based on this fact: The light from heaven
> came into the world, but they loved the darkness more than the
> light, for their actions were evil. They hate the light because
> they want to sin in the darkness. They stay away from the
> light for fear their sins will be exposed and they will be pun-
> ished. But those who do what is right come to the light gladly,
> so everyone can see that they are doing what God wants."*
> (John 3:19-21)

Supernatural Wonders

On one occasion as Jesus walked beside the Sea of Galilee, He
saw two brothers who were casting out their nets into the
lake. Jesus told them to follow Him and He would make them
fishers of men. At once, they left their nets and followed Him.
From there, He saw two more fishermen preparing their nets
and when Jesus called them, they immediately left their boat

and also followed Him. He began recruiting a group of men who would be His first disciples.

When He had called His twelve disciples to Him, He gave them power to heal all kinds of sickness and disease. As Jesus and His disciples began their journey together they came across a man who had demons for a long time and he wore no clothes nor did he have a house to live in but he lived in the tombs.

> As soon as he saw Jesus, he shrieked and fell to the ground before him, screaming, "Why are you bothering me, Jesus, Son of the Most High God? Please, I beg you, don't torture me!" For Jesus had already commanded the evil spirit to come out of him. This spirit had often taken control of the man. Even when he was shackled with chains, he simply broke them and rushed into the wilderness, completely under the demon's power. (Luke 8: 28-29)

The demons immediately recognized Jesus as the Son of God. The people who witnessed this exorcism were amazed and asked each other what kind of power this was. Jesus gave orders to evil spirits and they obeyed Him! The news Jesus had authority over demons as well as sicknesses and diseases rapidly spread throughout the whole region.

One day Jesus and many of His disciples entered a city where a large crowd had gathered. As he came near the city a dead man was being carried out, the only son of a widow. When the Lord saw her, He said to her "Don't cry."

Then he walked over to the coffin and touched it, and the bearers stopped. "Young man," he said, "get up." Then the dead boy sat up and began to talk to those around him! (Luke 7: 13-15)

The news of a man being raised from the dead and many other supernatural events caused great crowds to follow Him. On another occasion He went up on a mountainside and sat down to teach. He declared joy would be given to those who shared in the redemption of the Kingdom of God. He proclaimed He came not to abolish the Law of the Prophets, but to fulfill them. He told them "not the smallest letter nor the stroke of a pen would disappear from the Law until everything was accomplished". He taught many subjects including murder, adultery, divorce, oaths, loving your enemies and giving to the needy. He spoke of prayer and fasting, worries, and judging others. Jesus taught them about ethics and principles of the laws instead of the specific Jewish regulations twisted into legalist tradition. He presented moral living so high it presented a new standard for living. Jesus made many proclamations about the Kingdom of God coming to the earth through Him.

Threatened by His Power and Authority

As Jesus and His disciples traveled throughout the region He taught in parables and prophesied which fulfilled more prophecies. People reached out to touch Him because of the healing power He displayed. He healed the blind, the deaf and the crippled. He cast demons out of many people, restoring them to health and a full life. He raised people from the dead. He had command over nature and calmed storms, walked on water and fed thousands of people supernaturally. The supernatural powers He exhibited were phenomenal and because of these, many believed He was the promised Messiah and the Son of God.

The Jewish leaders were very intimidated by His power and authority. They knew they were losing their dominance over the people due to this man's influence. In an attempt to retain their position, they tried to trick Jesus with difficult questions concerning Jewish laws and prophecies. They wanted to catch Jesus making a mistake, damaging His credibility and persuasion among the Jewish people. One man asked Jesus which was the greatest commandment in the Law. Jesus told him "To love the Lord your God with all your heart, strength, soul and mind". This was the first and greatest commandment. The second was like the first, "Love your neighbor as yourself". He explained to them all the law and the prophets hung on these two commandments. He always had the right answer, but the leaders of the Jews continued to plot against Jesus. When He performed miracles the Jewish leaders accused Him of using demonic power to perform His miracles. If He healed someone on the Sabbath, they accused Him of disobeying Jewish law, for no one was to work on the Sabbath. They did everything in their power to stop Jesus from influencing the Jewish people.

Fulfillment of Prophecy

Jesus told His disciples that the Son of Man (which is what He often called Himself) must go to Jerusalem and suffer many things. He would be rejected by the elders, chief priests and teachers of the law. They would condemn Him and give Him over to the Gentiles to be mocked, flogged and crucified. He proclaimed on the third day after His death, He would be raised back to life.

Even though all of these events were the fulfillment of prophecy, the disciples were dismayed and overcome with grief. They could not believe their Master was going to die in such a horrible manner. Jesus prepared the disciples for His coming suffering and death. He comforted them by explaining He would eventually come back in His Father's glory with the angels, and then He would reward each person according to what they had done. He reminded them of the prophecies written long before his suffering. It was God's plan of salvation for mankind.

He was despised and rejected- a man of sorrows, acquainted with bitterest grief. We turned our backs on him and looked the other way when he went by. He was despised, and we did not care. Yet it was our weaknesses he carried; it was our sorrows that weighed him down. And we thought his troubles were a punishment from God for his own sins! But he was wounded and crushed for our sins. He was beaten that we might have peace. He was whipped, and we were healed! (Isaiah 53: 3-5).

All Jesus explained to His disciples concerning the events that would happen to Him, was the fulfillment of many prophecies the prophets had spoken hundreds of years beforehand. Jesus came specifically to endure suffering on the cross for the sins of all people. His death symbolically portrayed the animal sacrifice under the old covenant and would provide forgiveness for sin once and for all.

The King on the Cross

The time came for Jesus to give His life as a sacrifice, to pay the price for the sins of mankind. This had to happen for God is a just God. The price for sin had to be paid, and only the sinless blood of Jesus would be a sufficient payment to redeem the human race. Mankind would be reconciled to God through the death of His Son.

Through Adam sin and death came to the human race. Christ, as the "second Adam" brought universal blessing to mankind through one righteous act. Just as sin entered the world through one man, the one act of righteous sacrifice brought justification through faith for all men. The Son of God came as a man. His perfect obedience was necessary, in order that man might be saved through a perfect sacrifice for sin. The law of God had to be fulfilled through Christ, for no man could see God's face unless he is perfected in righteousness by the blood of Christ. Christ's righteousness would be credited to those who would believe. The promises and prophecies God had spoken beforehand regarding His son Jesus Christ's first coming were now almost fully accomplished.

Jesus was betrayed, arrested and forsaken, just as He told His disciples He would be. The leaders of the Jews seized Him and charged Him with the crime of blasphemy. They turned Jesus over to the Roman authorities who could not find any crime He had committed. The chief priests and rulers of the Jews persuaded the Roman governor to crucify Him anyway.

They hung Jesus on a cross by piercing His hands and feet with nails.

By this time it was noon, and darkness fell across the whole land until three o'clock. The light from the sun was gone. And suddenly, the thick veil hanging in the Temple was torn apart. Then Jesus shouted, "Father, I entrust my spirit into your hands!" And with those words he breathed his last. (Luke 23: 44-46)

At that moment the earth shook and the rocks split. They took His body and wrapped it in linen cloth and placed it in a tomb cut in the rock and rolled a stone before the entrance. The Roman soldiers made the tomb secure by putting a seal on the stone and posting guards, for the Jewish leaders had heard Jesus was supposed to rise from the grave. They did not want to take any chances someone would come and take his body and claim that He had been resurrected.

Conquering Death

On the third day after Jesus was crucified some of His followers went to the tomb where He lay. There was a great earthquake; for an angel of the Lord came down from heaven and going to the tomb, rolled back the stone and sat on it. His appearance was like lightning, and his clothes were white as snow. The guards were so afraid of him that they shook and became like dead men.

Then the angel spoke to the women. "Don't be afraid!" he said. "I know you are looking for Jesus, who was crucified. He isn't here! He has been raised from the dead, just as he said would happen. Come, see where his body was lying. (Matthew 28:5-6)

As the women hurried away from the tomb, afraid yet filled with joy, Jesus met them. They came to Him, clasped His feet and worshipped Him. Then Jesus said to them, "Do not be afraid. Go and tell my brothers to go to Galilee there they will see me". The woman ran ahead and told the disciples what they had just witnessed. After hearing the women's story the disciples headed quickly to Galilee to see if Jesus was really alive. Suddenly Jesus himself was standing there among them.

The whole group was startled and frightened, thinking they were seeing a ghost! "Why are you frightened?" he asked. "Why are your hearts filled with doubt? Look at my hands. Look at my feet. You can see that it's really me. Touch me and make sure that I am not a ghost, because ghosts don't have bodies, as you see that I do." As he spoke, he showed them his hands and his feet. Still they stood there in disbelief, filled with joy and wonder. Then he asked them, "Do you have anything here to eat?" They gave him a piece of broiled fish, and he ate it as they watched.

Then he said, "When I was with you before, I told you that everything written about me in the law of Moses and the prophets and in the Psalms must be fulfilled." Then he opened their minds to understand the Scriptures. And he said, "Yes, it was written long ago that the Messiah would suffer and die and rise from the dead on the third day. It was also written that this message would be proclaimed in the authority of his name to all the nations, beginning in Jerusalem: 'There is forgiveness of sins for all who repent.' You are witnesses of all these things.

"And now I will send the Holy Spirit, just as my Father promised. But stay here in the city until the Holy Spirit comes and fills you with power from heaven." (Luke 24:37-49)

Jesus was indeed alive and had conquered death! Jesus showed Himself in His resurrected state for a number of days; at the empty tomb, to two men on the road to Emmaus, to Peter, to the disciples and eventually to more than five hundred. His body was in a glorified state. He was with them on earth in His resurrected state for forty days and continued to teach them about the Kingdom of God. He told His apostles to stay in Jerusalem and wait for the gift that God promised. John had baptized with water, but they were to be baptized with the Holy Spirit. His followers asked Him if He was going to restore the kingdom of Israel. He told them it was not for them to know the times or dates the Father had set by His own authority. He said they would receive power when the Holy Spirit came to them, and they would be His witnesses in Jerusalem and to the ends of the earth.

Jesus was taken up into heaven and a cloud hid Him from their sight. They were looking intently up into the sky as He was ascending, when suddenly two angels stood beside them. They asked the disciples why they stood there looking into the sky. The angels told them Jesus, who ascended into heaven, would come back in the same way He went into heaven.

It Is Finished

The death of Jesus Christ was the supreme and final payment for the sins of humanity. The resurrection of Jesus Christ was a mighty supernatural declaration He was indeed the true Messiah and had conquered death.

Jesus was crucified and was made the sacrificial lamb whose sinless life was given so salvation would be available to all. Christ died for the sins of everyone throughout all generations, but only those who choose to believe this receive the benefits of that sacrifice. Anyone who truly believes that Jesus is the Son of God and asks Him to forgive their sins and invites Him to live inside of them is born again of the Spirit. Receiving Christ involves turning to God from self, living by faith in God, and trusting in His Word. For it is impossible to please God without faith. By grace, mankind has been saved through their faith; it is the free gift of God and not a result of works.

Jesus taught no one could see the Kingdom of God unless they were "born again." This seemed puzzling because many could not understand how they could be born twice. Jesus explained a person is born of water, which was the first birth, and then of the Spirit which is the second birth. The flesh gives birth to flesh, but the Spirit gives birth to spirit. The Holy Spirit comes to live inside of us regenerating the dead spirit we are all born with, when by faith a person believes. Through the new or second birth, a person goes through divine transformation and made a partaker of a new nature. Once Jesus lives inside of someone, they go through a transformation, because of this new nature. They begin to die to their old sinful ways and receive the righteousness Christ brings into their lives.

The blood of Jesus washes away mankind's sin in God's eyes. The gift of eternal life in heaven with God was made available to all mankind.

> *"For God so loved the world that he gave his only Son, so that everyone who believes in him will not perish but have eternal life. God did not send his Son into the world to condemn it, but to save it. (John 3:16-17)*

From the beginning, God had a plan to triumph over sin and evil. God's victory was given through the Lord Jesus Christ's blood. This victory was a testimony;

> *And I am convinced that nothing can ever separate us from his love. Death can't, and life can't. The angels can't, and the demons can't. Our fears for today, our worries about tomor-*

row, and even the powers of hell can't keep God's love away.
Whether we are high above the sky or in the deepest ocean,
nothing in all creation will ever be able to separate us from
the love of God that is revealed in Christ Jesus our Lord.
(Romans 8:38-39)

Jesus' first earthly mission was fulfilled and He provided a way for all humanity to be reconciled to God. He also destroyed the works of the Devil, giving humans a way to have victory over the powers of darkness.

The age of grace had begun and now the blood of Christ provided forgiveness to all mankind. Man could not earn this through his own effort, nor could he ever live a life without sin, "for all have sinned and fall short of the glory of God". Christ's supreme and final payment for the sins of humanity frees those who receive Him and brings them out from under the curse of the law and slavery to sin. God graciously adopts all believers as His sons and daughters.

God not only revealed His plan to mankind, but also prepares His people to help Him accomplish His purpose. God's grand design was to bring a group of eternally lost people into eternal life with Him. In order to complete His work of salvation, God became personally involved in the world, sending His only Son. In Christ, God personally revealed Himself in human flesh.

Praise the Lord from the heavens! Praise him from the skies!
Praise him all his angels! Praise him all the armies of heaven
Praise him, sun and moon! Praise him all you twinkling stars!
Praise him, skies above! Praise him, vapors high above the
clouds! His orders will never be revoked.

(Psalm 148: 1-6)

Chapter Nine

THE NEW WEAPON

J ust before Jesus left the earth and ascended into heaven, He directed the apostles to return to Jerusalem and wait for the gift God has promised to give them. Jesus explained that John had baptized with water but they would be baptized with the Holy Spirit.

But when the Holy Spirit has come upon you, you will receive power and will tell people about me everywhere- in Jerusalem, throughout Judea, in Samaria, and to the ends of the earth."
(Acts 1:8)

They returned to Jerusalem and gathered in an upper room where they joined together constantly in prayer.

Suddenly, there was a sound from heaven like the roaring of a mighty windstorm in the skies above them, and it filled the house where they were meeting. Then what looked like flames or tongues of fire appeared and settled on each of them. And everyone present was filled with the Holy Spirit and began

speaking in other languages, as the Holy Spirit gave them this
ability. (Acts 2: 2-4)

The Holy Spirit had immediately empowered them to speak in languages they had not previously learned! The power Jesus promised to send had arrived. This was the Holy Spirit baptism.

There were people from many nations in Jerusalem on that day for the celebration of the Passover. When the foreigners heard unusual sounds coming from the upper room a crowd gathered together bewildered and amazed. They were baffled to find people coming from an upper room speaking in other languages and some who spoke in their own dialect, proclaiming boldly Jesus Christ was indeed the son of God. Because the foreigners knew these men and women were simple ordinary people, they asked how it was possible to hear them speak in their own languages. Others, who had not understood any of the tongues, and saw them acting "drunk" made fun of them, saying they must have had too much wine to drink even though it was early in the morning.

Peter, one of Christ's apostles, was filled with the Holy Spirit and began speaking out with a new- found boldness. He began proclaiming to the crowds Jesus was a man credited by God to them through miracles, wonders and signs God did through Him. Peter spoke of God's set purpose and foreknowledge giving Jesus to the world. Wicked men put

Jesus to death by nailing Him to a cross. God had raised Him from the dead, freeing Him from the agony of death, because it was impossible for death to keep its hold on Jesus. There were many witnesses to this fact. Peter shared how Jesus was resurrected and sitting at the right hand of God exalted. Having received from the Father the promise of the Holy Spirit, he poured out what they saw and heard that day.

When the crowds who had gathered outside the upper room heard this, they were cut to the heart and asked the apostles what to do. They were admonished to believe, repent and be baptized in the name of Jesus Christ for the forgiveness of their sins and they would also receive the gift of the Holy Spirit. This promise was for them and their children. On that day, about three thousand people were added to the number of those who believed Jesus was indeed the Messiah.

This was the beginning of the Church of Jesus Christ. Everyday, thousands more believed when they heard about Jesus, especially as they witnessed the power His followers displayed healing people and casting our devils. People throughout the region were deeply touched by the miracles the Holy Spirit empowered believers to perform and the boldness of their preaching. Groups of those who became believers joined together with other believers to pray, study, and worship their newfound Savior. The people who believed were later called Christians, which means Christ- like, because through the power of the Holy Spirit, Jesus was now living inside of them giving them a new divine nature. They sincerely desired to be like Christ; pure and sinless. They had been born again of the Spirit.

Some people, astonished to see miracles, believed it was sorcery or magic making these things happen. The apostles proclaimed they were not able to perform these miracles by their own power, but by the God of Abraham, Isaac & Jacob. The same God of their forefathers glorified Jesus, His Son. It was the name of Jesus and faith in Him that healed and set them free from the bondage of demonic power.

The Comforter and Teacher

Before Jesus came to earth, the Holy Spirit also came upon mankind at times and provided supernatural knowledge or power to those who God used for His purposes. Now that Jesus had come to Earth as a human, died, and was resurrected, He opened the door for Holy Spirit to come into all of those who believed.

Holy Spirit is characterized by truth. He brings people to the understanding of God and works relentlessly at leading people to Jesus. He also convicts us of sin. He is the great Comforter and Teacher, empowering each individual believer with supernatural gifts. When a person is filled with the Holy Spirit, the indwelling Spirit of Christ is able to rule in the minds and bodies of individuals. The solution to sin did not lie in a code of ethics people were exhorted to obey, but rather by God's gift of the Holy Spirit.

The priests, rulers, elders and teachers of the Jewish law were greatly disturbed because the apostles continued to proclaim Jesus had been resurrected from the dead and thousands had become believers. In order to stop this movement from spreading any further among the people, they sternly warned the Christians not to speak to anyone in the name of Jesus. They even began arresting the believers thinking this would stop them from professing Jesus as the Messiah. These Disciples of Christ refused to submit to the Jewish leader's demands and boldly refused because they could not help speaking about what they had seen and heard.

More and more people believed in the Lord and the Church was growing very fast. As a result, more people brought the sick into the streets and laid them on beds and mats so they could be healed. The crowds grew in number as people gathered together. They brought those tormented by evil spirits and all of them were delivered. Day after day in the temple courts and from house to house, they never stopped teaching and proclaiming the good news Jesus was the Savior of the world.

The infant Church emerged from Jerusalem ready to stand in the face of pagan Rome with its military might and atheistic Greece's philosophical might. The Church grew to convert the uncivilized people held in the clutches of witchcraft and idolotry. The early church knew a spiritual battle must ensue and used the gifts of the Spirit to overcome the powers of darkness. Without the power of the Holy Spirit, the Church was helpless before the onslaught of the world, the flesh, and the devil.

The Holy Spirit brought three gifts of revelation; words of wisdom, words of knowledge and discerning of spirits. In addition, there are three gifts of power; the gift of faith, the gift of working miracles, and the gift of healing. There are also three gifts of inspiration; the gift of prophecy, the gift of speaking in various tongues, and the gift of interpretation of tongues.

The spiritual gifts God armed the church with were to be used to defeat any enemy that would come against it. They were divine communications transmitted from heaven through the Holy Spirit to the Church of the Lord Jesus Christ.

Jesus came to earth to redeem mankind and to conquer the powers of evil. His works functioned in the framework of the gifts of the Spirit. Jesus was directed, guided and ener-gized by the Holy Spirit. When the same Holy Spirit came to the Church, they believed they were able to do the same works Jesus did and even greater works. Christ was alive and seated at the right hand of God, the position of power, interceding for His Body of Believers.

The devil had counterfeits for anything of value God brought to the Church. He sought to counterfeit all of the nine gifts of the Holy Spirit. Psychics sought to reveal the future and witches to heal by potions and curses with hexes and incantation. Palm reading and fortune telling were attempts to know present and future supernaturally. Tools like Quija boards and Tarot cards were used to communicate with demonic sources. These were all a counterfeit of God's beautiful gift of miracles. Satan's attempts to deceive mankind were disguised as acts to benefit mankind, just as he himself was transformed into an "angel of light" by his deception.

The Door is Open

The Jewish leaders caused a great persecution to break out against the early church at Jerusalem and Christians were scattered throughout the land. Those who had been dispersed preached the good news about Jesus and the Kingdom of God wherever they went. When people heard and saw the miraculous signs that followed them, they paid close attention to what they shared. Evil spirits came out of many. Paralytics and cripples were healed. More and more people became believers.

There was one more important message the early disciples were given to teach people. Through the death and resurrection of Jesus Christ the barrier between the Jew and the Gentile had been removed. The Jewish people were no longer the only people to whom God would have a relationship. God did not favor an individual because of his station in life, his nationality or his material possessions; He loved all of His children. The Jewish believers were compelled to recognize God was going to save Gentiles on equal terms with Jews. By divine action rather than by human choice, the door was opened to Gentiles. The Gentiles had received the same spiritual gifts as the Jewish believers. For instance some spoke in tongues, as did some of the Jewish Christians when the Holy Spirit came. It was always God's plan that all men would be saved and come into a relationship with Him.

This new teaching caused great division in the Jewish community. They had been the only humans God had communicated through. They were the ones chosen to receive the law and the prophets. It was difficult for some of them to share their God with the world.

The old covenant with the system of sacrifices for atonement or the covering of sin was gone. No longer did the Jews who believed in Jesus have to cut the throats of an animal and apply that blood to be payment for their sins. The practice of circumcision was no longer necessary. The new covenant was in effect now that Jesus had come to earth. Now each individual could have an intimate relationship with God because Jesus had provided a bridge to cover the gap sin had put between mankind and God.

This is how God planned it from the beginning. He loved His creation and wanted to spend every day intimately involved in their lives. He provided a plan for salvation and forgiveness of sin. Satan thought he could separate mankind from God forever.

Building a Sure Foundation

The church continued to grow. The good news of God's Kingdom brought by Jesus Christ spread throughout the earth. Armies could not destroy this amazing Church; Governments could not enforce laws to control it. Courts could not pass edicts to stop it. The strongest evil forces forged by the devil and the ingenious minds of perverted men could not command or destroy the Church of Jesus Christ.

The spiritual battles were ongoing and the conflict between the forces of evil, between light and darkness; between men who served Jesus and men who served Satan was very real. Three powerful enemies were constantly trying to defeat the Christian: the world's system, the person's flesh, and the devil's forces. The key to conquering the world is the love of the Father. Victory over the flesh is through the Holy Spirit. Power over the devil is the name, the Word and the blood of Jesus Christ the Son of God.

It is the Lord who laid the foundations of the earth and determined its measurements. He laid its cornerstone while the morning stars sang together. He shuts the sea with doors and causes the dawn to know its place. He enters the springs of the sea and walks in its depths. He enters the treasury of snow and hail and knows the ordinances of the heavens.

Part Four

PEACE ON EARTH

Chapter Ten

DESTINY REVEALED

Before Jesus left earth, He confirmed the prophecies from times past that predicted a great defeat against Israel, even the destruction of the temple. He shared the fore-knowledge Israel would fall to her enemies and just like all holy prophecy, it became a reality. The Romans completely destroyed Jerusalem and the temple buildings about seventy years after Jesus was resurrected. This was an ongoing cycle with the nation of Israel order, disorder and reorder. After this great defeat, almost two thousand years passed before God intervened on behalf of the nation of Israel again.

God promised His chosen people a Messiah, a Savior, and yet many of the Jewish people failed to believe Jesus was this promised One. The Jews zeal for God was authentic and genuine, but so many of them did not have the revelation, that the detailed prophecies prophets wrote over the centuries about the coming Messiah, were all fulfilled through Jesus Christ. The sin of disbelief continued to separate the Jews from walking fully with God. God warned them in the Scripture when he said,

"I am placing a stone in Jerusalem that causes people to stumble, and a rock that makes them fall. But anyone who believes in him will not be disappointed. (Romans 9: 33)

After the Romans destroyed Jerusalem, the remaining Jewish people where scattered among the nations. Because of their disobedience they lived without a homeland, subject to the strongest racial prejudice and torment suffered by any people group.

For the Lord will scatter you among all the nations from one end of the earth to the other. There you will worship foreign gods that neither you nor your ancestors have known, gods made of wood and stone! (Deuteronomy 28: 64)

Signs of the End of the Age

As the years and centuries passed, the population on earth grew immensely and many different nations emerged, as well as many different cultures. World powers and governments surfaced and then collapsed. Time and time again authority and power was handed over to the next nation whose military might had won another war. Thousands of years passed and the land Israel had occupied was ruled by many different nations.

Multitudes continued to join the Church and as it grew, the good news Jesus was the Savior of the world was written down and taught to many people near and far. Generation after generation this message of love for the human race was passed along and embraced, despite the persecution the dark forces of the earth unleashed against it.

Satan was continually planting false doctrine and religious beliefs in the hearts and minds of people. Religions that exalted false gods were birthed out of the many different nations and cultures of the world. Counterfeit teachings and imitations of the true Christ were deceiving millions of people. As religious deception continued, conflicts increased as the world looked for religious or political answer to the world's problems. Some churches took God's Word and either added or subtracted from it creating religions that taught distorted truth. Others embraced inaccurate world religions established centuries before Jesus came, when the prophets were crying out that God loved the world and was going to send a Savior. There were even those who chose to believe there was no God and all creation had just evolved by chance. Jesus warned of many false teachers who would deceive mankind and cause the truth to be denied. Humanity reached out for God, but stumbling and choosing deceptions. Religion was a very successful weapon Satan used to bring hate and confusion into the world.

The Rebirth of a Nation

Religion has always played a major role in the history of the world. Many of the wars in mankind's history were caused by religious, political or ethnic conflicts. In the twentieth century a nation called Germany became very mighty, having one of the most powerful armies on earth. Their leader, Adolph Hitler, was determined to exterminate the Jewish people. This persuasive man convinced much of his nation hatred for the Jews was justified and they must be annihilated. This mighty nation, with its powerful military forces, began to terrorize the Jews and millions of them were tortured and put to death. There were other powerful nations who allied themselves in opposition against this corrupt man and his armies which brought World War II on earth. Eventually, this evil man and his armies were defeated and the mass murder of the Jews was put to an end. Once this perverted, demonic power had been conquered, the horrors of this Holocaust produced some sympathy for the Jewish people. The state of Israel was reestablished so Jews would have a homeland after two thousand years of being disbursed around the world. Israel would once again be an independent nation with Jews living on a portion of the land that God had given to them thousands of years before through Abraham.

The re-establishment of Israel as a nation was the most significant prophetic sign concerning the Second Coming of

Jesus Christ. Jesus said He would return and described the signs that would indicate the time was near. There were written prophecies which declared Israel had to experience a "rebirth" before the return of the Messiah. The prophets had proclaimed this nation would be born in one day, and it was. For centuries people who heard or read this prophecy in Gods written Word had questioned and wondered how it would be possible for a nation to be born in one day. This prophecy, like all of the others that seemed impossible, came to pass because God had declared it would happen.

> "Instead they will say, 'As surely as the Lord lives, who brought the people of Israel back to their own land from the land of the north and from all the countries to which he had exiled them.' For I will bring them back to this land that I gave their ancestors. (Jeremiah 16: 15)

Jesus taught His disciples there would be an end to the church age and at that time He was coming back to rule over the earth. They had asked Him for the signs of these times. The disciples wanted to know what would be the indication of His second coming and of the end of the age. Jesus explained that when Israel became a nation, it should be obvious to all He was returning soon. The generation that witnessed the rebirth of Israel, would be the final generation of the age. Prophecy also declared Jerusalem would not be under Gentile rule in this generation, a situation that existed since her fall to Rome. The time had come when the Jewish people would rule the nation of Israel and recapture the city of Jerusalem. The Gentiles were no longer in control of God's holy city.

> *They will be brutally killed by the sword or sent away as captives to all the nations of the world. And Jerusalem will be conquered and trampled down by the Gentiles until the age of the Gentiles come to an end. (Luke 21: 24)*

Once the nation of Israel had been reestablished, Jewish people from around the world began returning to their homeland by the hundreds of thousands. Prophets had long before written many Jews would return to Israel before the Messiah returned. The return of millions of Jews to Israel was another prophetic sign the end of the age was near.

> *I will firmly plant them there in the land I have given them,"* Says the Lord your God. *"Then they will never be uprooted again."* (Amos 9: 15)

Jesus prophesied this generation who saw these events happen would certainly not pass away, but they would be the people who would be living when Jesus came back to get His Church. He was telling them what was going to happen ahead of time so that, even though they did not know the day and the hour, they would know the season of His return.

And wars will break out near and far, but don't panic. Yes, these things must come, but the end won't follow immediately. The nations and kingdoms will proclaim war against each other, and there will be famines and earthquakes in many parts of the world. (Matthew 24: 6-7)

The history of man is a story of never ending violence, with one tribe or nation pitted against another seeking to dominate or control territory, food supplies, riches or power. So yes, there were wars and rumors of wars throughout the centuries. But the difference was wars were occurring much more frequently all over the earth, with significantly more powerful weapons being used.

The planet always had a certain amount of earthquakes, tsunamis, volcanoes and natural disasters, but they were substantially increasing in frequency and intensity. Incurable diseases, famines and widespread pestilence were more indications Jesus was soon returning. Diseases were occurring that affected millions of people and spread rapidly all over the world; some of them with no known cure.

There will be great earthquakes, and there will be famines and epidemics in many lands, and there will be terrifying things and great miraculous signs in the heavens. (Luke 21: 11)

All of these sufferings were "trumpet blasts" from the throne of God to the people on earth they were the last generation before the return of the Messiah. Prophecy indicated the persecution of Christians would intensify and they would be hated by all nations because of their belief Jesus was the only way to know the one true God. Many turned away from their faith, betraying and hating each other. Because of the increase of wickedness, the love of many grew cold, but those who stood firm to the end were saved.

An Explosion of Knowledge

At this same point in history, there was another dramatic change happening on earth. Since the Garden of Eden, mankind's transportation was limited to walking or using horses. They only had light at night by way of candle or oil lamps. The manner in which people farmed, ate, traveled, and communicated had remained unchanged. In the span of decades mankind invented electricity, automobiles, computers, and even traveled to the moon and other planets. Their technology increased exponentially. Knowledge and information was made available to them at the press of a button. An explosion of knowledge occurred rapidly and life was vastly different for this generation more than any other. A prophet wrote that at the end of the age, a great increase of knowledge would happen as a sign of the Second Coming of Christ.

"But you, Daniel, keep this prophecy a secret; seal up the book until the time of the end. Many will rush here and there, and knowledge will increase."(Daniel 12: 4)

Prophecy also taught the entire globe would simultaneously be able to see the same things happening. No generation could explain this concept until the time period in history when television, satellites and wireless communication became a reality. Virtually the entire world had access to the same information as an event happened anywhere on earth.

Because of the increase in knowledge, mankind now invented weapons of destruction that were capable of destroying the whole world. The destructive capabilities of war increased to a degree never before considered possible. The age old struggle for land, power and money became much more frightening because of man's incredible ability to destroy the earth's population. These weapons explained this prophecy;

And the Lord will send a plague on all the nations that fought against Jerusalem. Their people will become like walking corpses, their flesh rotting away. Their eyes will shrivel in their sockets, and their tongues will decay in their mouths. (Zachariah 14:12)

Nuclear weapons humans invented were fully capable of accomplishing these horrific results. Mankind had never been capable of reaping such devastation on each other in times prior to the Industrial and Technological revolutions of the 20th century.

Great Deception

This powerful end time communication technology enabled the truth of God's word to be broadcast throughout the whole world so virtually every person would have the opportunity to hear God's words and embrace or reject them.

Prophecy declared deception would be epidemic on the earth in the time of the last generation, just before Jesus returned. For centuries, mankind had been weakening their will with lies. At the end of the age secular humanism was embraced and man thought he could assume the role of God. People taught on "situational ethics", embracing the philosophy there was no absolute right or wrong. New Age theories deceived people into believing they themselves were gods. Environmental religions based in witchcraft believed that the earth was "mother goddess" and worshipped the creation instead of the Creator. Satanism and teachings of occult practices deceived many with their demonic displays of power. Deception had always been a key part of Satan's warfare against man, but it become rampant in the world. Astrology, psychic phenomenon, witchcraft, and the occult permeated the world. New perversions of Christianity and world religions captured the attention of many. A world of superstition, fear, and demonic activity was deceiving millions of people.

They traded the truth about God for a lie. So they worshiped and served the things God created instead of the Creator himself, who is worthy of eternal praise! Amen. That is why God abandoned them to their shameful desires. Even the women turned against the natural way to have sex and instead indulged in sex with each other. And the men, instead of having normal sexual relations with women, burned with lust for each other. Men did shameful things with other men, and as a result of this sin, they suffered within themselves the penalty they deserved. Since they thought it foolish to acknowledge God, he abandoned them to their foolish thinking and let them do things that should never be done. Their lives became full of every kind of wickedness, sin, greed, hate, envy, murder, quarreling, deception, malicious behavior, and gossip. They are backstabbers, haters of God, insolent, proud, and boastful. They invent new ways of sinning, and they disobey their parents. They refuse to understand, break their promises, are heartless, and have no mercy. They know God's justice requires that those who do these things deserve to die, yet they do them anyway. Worse yet, they encourage others to do them, too. (Romans 1: 25-32)

In most cultures sins such as homosexuality and fornication were embraced in the name of "love" and personal choice. The laws of God were totally dismissed as myths forbidden in their governments and education systems. The world governments were filled with corruption and the world systems were deceitful. Despite all the signs the end of the age was near, billions of people turned from the truth and embraced the only thing that was left to accept; lies.

Jesus told His disciples no one would know the day or hour of the end of this age; not even the angels in heaven, nor Himself, but only God the Father. Those who listened saw the signs of His Second Coming. Many born again Christians understood the fulfillment of these prophecies indicating the end of the age.

To summarize what took place: First, Israel had become a nation and Jews from all over the world returned to their homeland. There was an explosion of knowledge and the ability to communicate worldwide. Thirdly, there was a great falling away from God and turning to human reasoning and a general global loss of moral values took place. Fourthly, there was great deception throughout the earth. In addition there was a great outpouring of incurable diseases. Natural disasters increased in frequency and severity as well as great signs in the heavens. There was even a global union of nations initiating a one-world government. Israel was surrounded by enemies who wanted to destroy her. Persecution of Christians was exponentially increasing.

The Great Plan

God is so full of grace. He wanted to reveal His plans to mankind so they would know what to expect, so they would understand His great plan for the redemption of mankind. Thousands of years before all of these events took place, He revealed what was going to happen through His inspired written Word. If any man would seek the Truth, the Holy Spirit would open up the eyes of their understanding so the Word of God would come alive to them and they would come to understand His great plan. He used prophets to predict the place and time of the first coming of Jesus and the ministry Jesus would have while on earth. They wrote about His suffering death and resurrection. God used prophets and His Son to explain the signs that would indicate the end of the age and the return of Christ. He used His inspired written Word to warn mankind about the spiritual warfare they would wage on earth and how to be victorious in these battles. He shared the truth with the human race and that truth could set them free from the bondage of sin and darkness that plagued the world. He told the world;

Ask me and I will tell you some remarkable secrets about what
is going to happen here. (Jeremiah 33:3)

However, very few chose to listen. Not many sought after these great mysteries He had revealed supernaturally to mankind.

The Christians who had learned about these prophecies through God's Word and understood it was the end of the age, tried to tell the world what was happening. They admonished the world to believe Jesus Christ was the Savior of the world and He was returning soon. Many laughed and continued in disbelief, living their lives in rebellion. It was just like in the days of Noah.

Satan and his evil forces of darkness were working overtime now, moving like never before on earth. They knew their time was limited. Likewise, there was a mighty move of God and the Holy Spirit was being poured out over the earth in a new and mightier way than ever before.

End Time Harvest

Hundreds of thousands of people gathered to be saved, healed and delivered. They experienced this great outpouring God had provided through the Holy Spirit for this last generation. Great churches with vast numbers of people worshipping God were established all over the world. Those who called themselves God's children were hard at work telling the whole world Jesus loved them and was soon returning to earth. Because of the technology available to them, they were able to broadcast the good news about Jesus Christ to the entire planet. Fulfilling prophecy;

And the Good News about the Kingdom will be preached throughout the whole world, so that all nations will hear it; and then, finally the end will come. (Matthew 24: 14)

Vast numbers of people heard the truth and as they taught God's Word, the Holy Spirit revealed to them the Bible was truly a love letter to the human race. They were convinced they needed to acknowledge their need for a Savior and believed Jesus died for their sins, defeated Satan and was now resurrected.

God graciously revealed many signs to indicate the return of Jesus to earth. Israel was the hour hand on the end time clock and Jerusalem was the minute hand indicating the divine timeline God had designed. Israel became a hated nation, surrounded by countries that wanted nothing more than to destroy her. The Muslim tribes living on the land given by God to the Jews always believed the Jews had taken the land that belonged to them. They continually attacked Israel to destroy her and reclaim the land. Muslims had a mosque in the city of Jerusalem that was holy to them and they wanted to once again rule over Jerusalem as they had in centuries before. Because of Israel's religious importance and her strategic significance, the nation had many other enemies as well. As time slipped closer to the consummation of the age, it seemed not only were the countries that surrounded Israel her enemies, but the whole world had turned against this nation God loved so much.

I will make Jerusalem and Judah like an intoxicating drink to all the nearby nations that send their armies to besiege Jerusalem. On that day I will make Jerusalem a heavy stone, a burden for the world. (Zechariah 12:2-3)

Israel always had an abundance of enemies because God had divinely appointed this nation to be a major part of His plan of redemption for mankind. The principalities and powers of evil were especially intent to destroy Israel, since this nation was used as a place for safekeeping of divine truth for generations. Through Israel, God gave the world the Word of God, the prophets, the apostles, and Jesus Christ. There would have been no Christianity without the Jewish contribution. God's love for Israel caused Satan's hatred for this nation and the Jewish people.

The human race was madly rushing towards a cataclysmic hour. Prophecy taught a global government and economy would be established at the end of the age. The necessary ingredients for a one- world government were in place for the first time in the history of civilization. A new international global organization seemed to be the solution for a world that could so easily destroy itself. The problems facing the world; nuclear war, terrorism, starvation, pestilence, pollution, and economic instability were international problems. Many global leaders and intellectuals believed a strong and effective world government was the only hope for survival of mankind on earth.

God's plan for mankind was unfolding, just as the prophets who were enlightened by the Holy Spirit had written it would. Holy prophecy proved beyond any reasonable doubt God knows the future and has chosen to share this knowledge with man through His Word, the Bible.

Let the sea and everything in it shout his praise! Let the earth and all living things join in. Let the rivers clap their hands in glee! For the Lord is coming to judge the earth. He will judge the world with justice, and the nations with fairness.

(Psalm 98: 7-9)

Chapter Eleven

THE MYSTERY

❧

People were eating, drinking, marrying, buying and selling on the day of the Rapture.

For since we believe that Jesus died and was raised to life again, we also believe that when Jesus returns, God will bring back with him the believers who have died. We tell you this directly from the Lord: We who are still living when the Lord returns will not meet him ahead of those who have died. For the Lord himself will come down from heaven with a commanding shout, with the voice of the archangel, and with the trumpet call of God. First, the Christians who have died will rise from their graves. Then, together with them, we who are still alive and remain on the earth will be caught up in the clouds to meet the Lord in the air. Then we will be with the Lord forever. (I Thessalonians 4:14-17)

As this mystical experience of being transported into the spiritual realm happened, all were given new, glorified, immortal bodies that would no longer know suffering, disease, pain, or death. In a moment's time, all the believers in Jesus the Messiah throughout the centuries were gathered in the heavens.

Receiving Crowns

This was also a time of judgment, when every believer stood before the Judgement Seat of Christ. It was here each one received what was due to them for what they had done with their lives as Christians. This judgement was not a matter of being saved or condemned; it was a matter of reward. All Christians were saved through their faith in Jesus Christ, not by their works. Everyone there received crowns, symbolizing their efforts on earth on God's behalf. Once they received their crowns, a great feast was prepared for the "Bride of Christ", the believers. This was a glorious celebration for those who had been victorious in their earthly life.

Meanwhile on earth, millions of Christians and children had simply vanished and there was chaos and great disorder over the entire planet. Massive problems were crippling the economies of the world. Drivers disappeared from airplanes, trains, buses, ships and automobiles. Men who were in positions of great authority in governments were gone. Military leaders and business executives had vanished. Many churches had no pastors or clergy left to minister to people who were filled with fear and bewildered because of this catastrophic event. People just vaporized in front of other people's eyes while they were talking, playing and working together. Millions were gone, but billions more remained. The world had never experienced anything of this magnitude and it profoundly affected every nation on earth. It was an event that brought the world together, making people simultaneously join in an effort for globalization and unity like never before.

The leaders of the nations attempted to explain the disappearance of millions from earth in various ways. One of the most accepted explanations was that aliens had abducted them because they were prohibiting world peace and unity with their Christian belief Jesus was the only way to God. For decades before the Rapture there had been a growing hype concerning aliens and unidentified flying objects from other planets. Thousands of people had witnessed strange objects in the heavens of unexplainable origin. People were entertained by various stories of technically advanced aliens coming to the earth to either destroy humans, or resolve their problems. So it was easy for them to accept this rationalization.

Most chose not to believe God had taken His elect up to the heavens, even though it had been prophesied this would happen in the ancient inspired writings of His prophets and apostles. Once again it was so easy for humans to be deceived.

The churches of the world were filled people weeping hysterically because they understood what happened. They knew the Church had been raptured and they had been left behind. Some read about this event in the Bible, others had heard of the rapture through Christians who had been proclaiming to the world that Jesus was coming back soon. Some of these who were left behind thought that they were Christians, but they had never truly been born again. They knew about Jesus in their mind, but they had never trusted Him and by faith believed He was Messiah, Savior of all. In each of their lives a believer had shared with them the teachings concerning this supernatural event called the Rapture, but many refused to believe, until they actually witnessed the disappearance of millions of people and they remembered what they had heard. Some of them who had studied God's prophetic words about the end time events knew of the terrible time coming and they would have to endure. Prophecy taught that after the Rapture, the most traumatic period in the history of the world would come. A time called the Great Tribulation.

Copycat Trinity

The Holy Spirit had been at work on earth restraining sin and now the church was gone. Satan thought he had the best shot he would ever have at taking God's place. Just as the one true God has existed for all eternity as Father, Son, and Holy Spirit, so the devil now created his own unholy twisted "trinity" which included Satan, the Beast and the False

Prophet. Satan's plan was to use this trio to compel the earth to worship him. Satan wanted to assume the place occupied by God in His program, the Beast was supposed to be the counterpart to Christ in the Holy Trinity and the ministry of the Holy Spirit was imitated by the False Prophet.

The Beast commonly known as the Antichrist was a powerful political leader who first revealed himself to the world as a great peace maker. The False Prophet was a man with extensive influence in the religious affairs of the world. Satan's plan was to use political and economic power to allow the Beast to become the dominant force in the world. The same pride and arrogance that caused Satan long ago to rebel against God was still the driving force behind his actions.

Prophecy taught the Antichrist would appear on the stage of the world after the Church was removed. Shortly after the rapture, he emerged from the part of the world known as Europe. God forewarned man this Antichrist would be a brilliant political leader with hypnotic charm, great intelligence and persuasiveness. First, he was a ruler over his own federation. Then, because he had inspired kingdoms at war to compromise on their conflicting issues, he became a renowned worldwide leader and proponent of peace. He seemed to have the answers for a troubled world; a leader who would enforce peace, present solutions to the world's problems, and bring unity to the people on earth. In his rise to power, he placed a hypnotic spell over each nation of the world until by their own consent they allowed him to rule the new federated empire. This man gained control over much of the world politically, economically and religiously. This all encompassing authority gave him power as no man had ever known in human history. His brilliance as a leader was superhuman, for he was directed by Satan himself. The Bible prophets taught with great detail where the Antichrist would come from, what he would attempt to accomplish, and how he would deceive many people.

A False Peace

At this time, the ongoing conflicts between Israel and her many enemies had the entire world in an uproar, causing division between many peoples and nations. The Antichrist formulated a peace plan for the Middle East the whole world wanted. He negotiated a seven- year peace treaty, guaranteeing Israel's security. The world was convinced there would be peace in Israel as last.

> He will make a treaty with the people for a period of one set of seven, but after half this time, he will put an end to the sacrifices and offerings. Then as a climax to all his terrible deeds, he will set up a sacrilegious object that causes desecration, until the end that has been decreed is poured out on this defiler. (Daniel 9:27)

Those who realized they had been left behind began learning what the Bible said concerning the future and started to strategize their survival. Prophecy showed them their time was very limited, for in seven years Jesus was coming back again to end these world conflicts and deliver Israel. It was urgent they used this window of time to share the good news of Jesus Christ as the only way of salvation to the remaining inhabitants of planet earth. As they watched the signing of the peace treaty with Israel, they knew what was to come. According to prophecy, this was the event that signified the beginning of the seven-year tribulation. They also understood the man who had established this peace treaty with Israel was the Antichrist. Those who comprehended what was going to happen realized the most awful time of catastrophe and destruction the world had ever known was at hand.

For the first three and one half years of the tribulation period the Antichrist continued his masquerade as a "prince of peace" and continued to seduce the nations into believing he would solve the world's problems. False prophets came onto the world scene and deception was like it had never been before. There were still many wars being fought, famines, pestilences, earthquakes and natural disasters intensified on the earth.

Christianity had been mocked before the Rapture and now with the Church gone, so was nearly all of the influence of His light on the world. Without the restraining presence of true believers, the false churches of the world combined into powerful religious and political institutions. This combined effort prepared the way for the new government that would have absolute power over the entire world. A new global religion was being embraced that taught every religion must be permitted all in the name of tolerance and love. Every belief was to be respected; every form of expression had to be allowed. Even the kings of the earth were mesmerized by this worldwide false religious system because it seemed it would bring peace to a world plagued with religious wars. Religions whose doctrine taught there was only one way to God were not tolerated. They were persecuted and silenced from sharing any teaching that did not embrace the theology there were many ways to God. The persecution of Christians greatly increased because they stood firm on their stance, Jesus is the only way to the one true God.

Jesus told him, "I am the way, the truth, and the life. No one can come to the Father except through me. (John 14:6)

The Mark of the Beast

One of the conditions to the seven- year peace treaty between Israel and the Antichrist allowed the Jewish people to rebuild their temple and to reestablish their ritual daily sacrifices. Since the orthodox Jews had not accepted the blood of Jesus as payment for all sin, they still believed the blood from animal sacrifices would cover their sin. The rebuilding of the Jewish temple caused great conflict in the Middle East. The nations both Muslim and non-Muslim surrounding Israel began to plan once again for the destruction of all Jewish people and the nation of Israel. Many world leaders formed a mighty coalition of soldiers and weapons. Three and one half years after the signing of the peace treaty nations to the north, south and east of Israel marched upon this Jewish nation with their powerful armies. As they had hoped, the Antichrist made no move to fulfill his peace treaty obligations to Israel.

You will come from your homeland in the distant north with your vast cavalry and your mighty army, and you will cover the land like a cloud. (Ezekiel 38:15-16)

As they were about to carry out their plan of annihilation, God stepped in with His mighty power.

God released His supernatural weapons against Israel's enemies beginning with a mighty earthquake that shook the earth with such violence that every army was stopped instantly. Many were buried alive. Next, God caused mass confusion to come upon these armies that came against Israel. These men turned their weapons against each other and many died by the weapon of his own brother. Finally, God allowed great floods of rain to be released as well as fire and brimstone which consumed the armies. These men who had come together to destroy Israel were almost entirely wiped out and the dead bodies of the invaders were strewn in the fields and mountains of Israel. Many died in this war and the burial of the dead took months.

God used this war against Israel for His own glory. He declared in His Word He would be known in the eyes of many nations. The only way to understand the significance of this incredible defeat was to accept it as an act of God. God supernaturally neutralized the enemies of Israel, as He had so many times in the past for them, that His name might be glorified. The earth was so full of so-called gods, by the time the true living God wiped out the enemies of Israel, there was no doubt that He was the only true God. Even though many came to understand who God really was through this war, there were many more with hardened hearts that chose not to believe God was in control.

The key reason God displayed His great power through this supernatural victory was to testify to His beloved Jewish people that He alone was their God. Through this miraculous deliverance the hearts of the Jewish people turned again to their God. However, a great portion of the Jewish people had not yet accepted Jesus as their Messiah. Because of this war, Israel's disastrous relationship with the Antichrist was abandoned and many began turning their affection back toward God.

With this war over, the real objective driving the Antichrist became apparent. Because of the dramatic weakening of the military forces of the nations that were defeated, the Antichrist decided it was time to extend his power and influence over the world. His goal was to initiate his one-world order. This was not difficult because the entire planet, with all of man's different religions and their many diverse cultures had been trying to bring the whole world together in unity. They were still determined this would save the world. The technology needed to accomplish this had now been established. The propaganda power of the world media and the blackmail power of international economic agreements made it possible for this world dictator to seize control of the world in a way that would have been impossible in any previous generation. This global effort promised peace and prosperity to all people.

First, the Antichrist broke his covenant with Israel by not doing anything to help them when the nations waged war against them. Next, he took the land of Israel and the temple in Jerusalem for himself. The temple was to serve as the focal point of the new religion he was offering the world and the new "trinity" the world would bow before. Also, this new commercial force would have a stronghold on the commerce and communication of the world. This religion he wanted to bring to the world was nothing less than the worship of Satan. Using the temple for sacrifices and observing the

Jewish people's customs was outlawed. Once the Antichrist seized the temple in Jerusalem, he became the center of world attention.

This supernatural power that Satan had given to the Antichrist was also given to his assistant the False Prophet. He made great signs on earth with this demonic power and fire came down from the heavens. These signs were called great and marvelous, deceiving many into believing he and the Antichrist were gods. Satan, the False Prophet and the Antichrist were joined together in their efforts to bring the worship of the people on earth to Satan. This False Prophet constructed a temple in the image of the Beast and he was able to give breath to this image so that it could speak like a man. This image had the ability to destroy those who would not worship the satanic trinity. It had supernatural life and death power. Most people bowed and worshipped this image because the world was convinced no one was like him and they believed no one could successfully make war against him.

As the Anti Christ implemented his plan for total control over the world's economy, he caused every person to receive a mark on their hand or forehead and no one could buy or sell except the ones who had this mark. This cash-less society where every financial transaction was electronically monitored was presented as a way to control criminals and terrorism. This mark was popular because it was a convenient

way to buy and sell with all financial and personal information on any individual being made available immediately.
This mark would eliminate the problem of missing people
because they could now track down the location of anyone,
anywhere on earth. Those who refused the mark were either
persuaded to concede or they were eliminated. Those who he
could not control or kill were without food, homes, and jobs.
Most people willingly received the mark of the Beast, with
the exception of the elect. God's Word gave a grave warning
to everyone that allowed the mark on their forehead or hands
it would mean eternal separation from Him. Receiving the
Mark of the Beast meant refusing Jesus and choosing to
worship Satan.

> Then a third angel followed them, shouting, "Anyone who
> worships the beast and his statue or who accepts his mark on
> the forehead or on the hand must drink the wine of God's an-
> ger. It has been poured out undiluted into God's cup of
> wrath. And they will be tormented with fire and burning
> sulfur in the presence of the holy angels and the Lamb. The
> smoke of their torment will rise forever and ever, and they
> will have no relief day or night, for they have worshiped the
> beast and his statue and have accepted the mark of his name."
> (Revelation 14:9-11)

This was the response of a righteous God to those who
refused His love and grace.

While Satan and his spiritual forces of wickedness were working hard at enforcing this one-world religion, government and economy, the wrath of God was beginning to be poured out onto the earth. The time had come for His righteous divine judgement on all of the nations of the world. Biblical prophecy foretold about three heavenly events, the Lord opening seven seals, angels blowing seven trumpets and angels pouring out seven bowls. Each of these succeeding events were judgments being released during that time called the Great Tribulation. These heavenly events would bring great catastrophes throughout the creation.

> *I watched as the Lamb broke the sixth seal, and there was a great earthquake. The sun became as dark as black cloth, and the moon became as red as blood. Then the stars of the sky fell to the earth like green figs falling from trees shaken by mighty winds. And the sky was rolled up like a scroll and taken away. And all of the mountains and all of the islands disappeared. (Revelation 6:12-14)*

Hail and fire destroyed one-third of the earth's vegetation, one-third of the sea had become defiled, and one-third of the rivers were contaminated with bitter water. One- third of the heavenly bodies were struck as stars fell from heaven with one-third of the light lost. Then came a terrible plague of locusts over the earth. They were given the power to torture mankind for five months. The agony people suffered from these locusts was like that of the sting of a scorpion. During those days men sought after death, but could not find it. The earth was quaking often and one-third of mankind had been killed by a plague of fire, smoke and sulfur. The sun turned black and the moon became as blood through the haze of destruction.

Many of those not killed by these plagues still did not repent of their evil works or worshipping demons and idols. They did not repent of their murders, magic arts, sexual immorality or wickedness.

Divine Judgment

True and just are God's judgments. The final hour of divine judgement had come over a world that would not allow Christ to reign. Those who had been marked by the Beast and worshipped his image were afflicted with ugly and painful sores. Next, the seas became filled with blood and every living thing in the sea died. The rivers and streams of the earth became unclean and the sun was given power to scorch the people on earth with fire. This intense heat seared them and they cursed the name of God, who sent these plagues, but they refused to repent and glorify Him. There was great pain inflicted on those who followed the Beast. Men gnawed their tongues in agony and cursed the God of heaven because of their pain and their sores.

Then the seventh angel poured out his bowl into the air, and a mighty shout came from the Throne of the Temple in heaven, saying "It is finished!" Then the thunder crashed and rolled, and lightning flashed. And there was an earthquake greater than ever before in human history. The great city of Babylon split into three pieces, and cities around the world fell into heaps of rubble. And so God remembered all of Babylon's sins, and he made her drink the cup that was filled with the wine of his fierce wrath. And every island disappeared, and all the mountains were leveled. There was a terrible hailstorm, and hailstones weighing seventy-five pounds fell from the sky onto the people below. (Revelation 16: 17-21)

During the last three and one half years of the Tribulation, Satan did have domination over the earth, but the world leaders had become discontent with Satan's dictatorship. They began challenging his world rule because the Antichrist was too powerful and untrustworthy. The Beast promised world peace and prosperity, but instead the world was experiencing massive catastrophes.

At the end of the Antichrist's reign, leaders of the South and leaders of the North came against the Antichrist like a whirlwind. Even though they had suffered great losses three and one half years prior during the war against Israel, they had vast resources of men and material and became a viable fighting force against the Antichrist. In addition to these rulers, came the leaders from the East advancing with an army two hundred million strong. They marched through the dried up bottom of the great river Euphrates to the very center of the Antichrist's empire. The greatest war of all history, involving hundreds of millions of men was set in motion in the valley of Megiddo.

Battle of Armageddon

Although from their point of view they were gathered to fight for world power, the armies of the world were actually assembled by Satan in anticipation of the Second Coming of Jesus as He returned from heaven. Satan actually believed he could stop Christ from taking over the earth. With the limited amount of supernatural power they had between them, the evil trinity prepared for the showdown against the Holy Trinity of God.

After hearing the news about the advancing eastern army, the Antichrist advanced to the place called Armageddon, to face the onslaught from the south, north and the east. His intention was to use the armies of the world as pawns for this final hour of victory. The armies of the world converged for a massive violent encounter.

Then I saw heaven opened, and a white horse was standing there. And the one sitting on the horse was named Faithful and True. For he judges fairly and then goes to war. His eyes were bright like flames of fire, and on his head were many crowns. A name was written on him, and only he knew what it meant. He was clothed with a robe dipped in blood, and his title was the Word of God. The armies of heaven, dressed in pure white linen, followed him on white horses. From his mouth came a sharp sword, and with it he struck down the nations. He ruled them with an iron rod, and he trod the winepress of the fierce wrath of almighty God. On his robe and thigh was written this title: KING OF KINGS AND LORD OF LORDS. (Revelation 19:11-16)

King of Kings

The Antichrist and the nations of the earth united their armies, instead of fighting each other, in an effort to stop Christ from taking authority over the earth. The armies gathered together to make war against Jesus, His angels and the saints. The entire military might of the world was not equipped to fight the great armies of heaven. Jesus set His feet on the Mount of Olives, east of Jerusalem. The Mount of Olives split in two from east to west forming a great valley, with half of the mountain moving north and half moving south. These armies were immediately defeated. God defended Israel because that is His covenant and Satan's time was up.

Jesus issued His spoken command and Satan, his demons, powers and principalities of spiritual wickedness were defeated. A plague struck the nations that fought against Jerusalem. Their flesh rotted while they were still standing on their feet, their eyes rotted in their sockets, and their tongues rotted in their mouths. The blood from this battle rose up to the height of a horse's bridle for about two hundred miles. All of this happened just as prophecy said it would. The annihilation of the armies that resisted Christ's return and waged war on Israel was God's righteous judgment on all nations.

The Antichrist was captured and with him the False Prophet who had performed the miraculous signs on his behalf. An angel came down from heaven with the key to the bottomless pit and a great chain in his hand. He took hold of Satan and locked him in the pit and set a seal on him, so that he would not be able to deceive the nations again until one thousand years were finished. Then he will be released again for a short while.

The Millennial Reign Begins

On that same day living water flowed out from Jerusalem, half to the eastern sea, and half to the western sea. Jesus became King over the whole earth!

At this time, all of the land south of Jerusalem became like the desert, but Jerusalem was raised up and remained in its place. The Jewish people, the chosen of God's covenant love were protected and redeemed. Jerusalem was inhabited by the Godly. Never again would enemies destroy her as Jerusalem was finally secure forever. It was prophesied thousands of years before, Christ's second return to earth would save Jerusalem and the nation of Israel from annihilation and would serve as the seat of His final Kingdom of justice.

In the aftermath of this battle, the Jewish people understood Jesus was truly their Messiah and He had come to save them. Now, the whole world bowed before Him, and every tongue confessed Jesus Christ was Lord, to the glory of God the Father. Jerusalem became the capital city from which Jesus Christ began His Millennial reign over the entire earth.

In the last days, the Temple of the Lord in Jerusalem will become the most important place on earth. People from all over the world will go there to worship. Many nations will come and say, "Come, let us go up to the mountain of the Lord, to the Temple of the God of Israel. There he will teach us his ways, so that we may obey him." For in those days the Lord's teaching and his word will go out from Jerusalem. The Lord will settle international disputes. All the nations will beat

their swords into plowshares and their spears into pruning
hooks. All wars will stop, and military training will come to
an end. (Isaiah 2:2-4)

The surviving people of the world were judged one by
one. First, all living Jews faced God. No one escaped this
judgement. The rebels, who had not accepted Jesus as their
Messiah prior to His Second Coming, were put to death. The
remaining believing Jews were allowed to enter the Promised Land as the first citizens of Christ's new Kingdom on
earth. The judgement of non-Jews happened next. The
Gentile population on earth appeared one by one before His
newly established throne in Jerusalem. Christ allowed those
who trusted Him, those who were saved by faith, to enter
the Millennial Kingdom. But those who did not believe in
Him, received eternal punishment. Those who were redeemed by the blood of Jesus entered the Millennium
Kingdom of Christ's reign on earth in their mortal bodies.
The Kingdom began with all unbelievers removed from the
earth. The entire adult population that remained had
experienced regeneration in their spirits through faith in
Christ.

Then the tribulation saints, including those that had died
as martyrs, were resurrected. All of these became priests of
Christ and reigned with Him.

Crossroads of the Ages

The beginning of Jesus' thousand year rule on earth was a crossroad of the ages. We now live on earth with Jesus as our King and enjoy a time of great peace. This Millennial age will last for one thousand years and then we will again enter another dispensation. For thousands of years prophets proclaimed the coming Messiah, who would be King over all of the nations and tribes of the earth, and would usher in the peace we now enjoy. Those prophecies have now been fulfilled.

The Lord looks down from heaven and sees the whole human race. From his throne he observes all who live on the earth. He made their hearts, so he understands everything they do.

(Psalm 33: 13-15)

Chapter Twelve

MILLINNIAL KINGDOM

The first time Jesus came to earth He came as a Lamb, a holy sacrifice for all of mankind. At that time, He brought redemption for all the forgiveness of sins and He destroyed the works of the devil. The second time Christ came to earth it was as King of kings and Lord of lords. As God had planned it from before creation, Jesus Christ is now ruling over the earth for one thousand years. Jesus now lives with us and His righteous Kingdom has been established forever. From the least of us to the greatest the earth is filled with the knowledge of the glory of the Lord!

During the seven-year tribulation the earth suffered great catastrophes and much of it had been destroyed. The planet was in total chaos from massive wars, famines, pestilences and judgments. When Christ came back to earth He personally supervised the process of regenerating the earth. The damage inflicted has been fully repaired and replenished. Jesus has restored the earth to what we now see and enjoy. He resettled our towns and the ruins have been rebuilt. The land has been rejuvenated with plentiful water and sunlight. The earth is once again abundantly fertile.

As in the former age we still plant crops, build houses and bear children. We are repopulating the earth. There are no wastelands, storms, droughts, crop failures or floods. Even the wild animals are tame and harmless and have stopped devouring each other. Now the lion eats straw like the ox, the cows graze with the bears and their young lie down together.

We live in a very different world from the prior age, for the old order of things has passed away and all things have become new. The original curse placed on creation back in the Garden of Eden has been removed. The ministry of Jesus as Healer and Redeemer is seen throughout the world.

His rule is absolute and just. All nations live in peace because He has established justice throughout the earth. For the first time in centuries, Jerusalem does not have to fear her enemies. Jesus is enforcing a one thousand-year treaty of perfect peace.

The Final Rebellion

Satan and his demonic forces are bound in the pit during this one thousand-year reign of Jesus, but we must remember they will be released for a short time when this age is at its end. He will once again inspire the nations to revolt against God.

All of humanity entered the Millennium righteous and repentant. Even though we do not have to battle Satan and his demons as human did in past ages, we still battle temptation as we are still partakers of the sin nature mankind is born with. Our flesh still desires the things that are not allowed by God and we all must experience regeneration of the spirit. The battle is still waging and when Satan is released he will have one last chance to take us and our children, and our children's children into eternal punishment with him, separated from God forever.

It is prophesied when Satan is released many will join with him in rebellion against God. As long as people are influenced by their sinful nature there will always be mockers and scoffers who reject God's authority. This millennial age is designed by God to be the final test of fallen humanity under the most ideal circumstances. All outward sources of temptation have been removed, so the true heart condition of each man can be determined.

Remember what happened to Satan and all of the fallen angels? They were all initially living in heaven with the Lord with no negative influences in a perfect environment when one-third of them decided to rebel against God. So just as a certain amount of angels decided to rebel against God in a perfect, heavenly environment, a certain number of human beings will do the exact same thing at the end of this Millennium Kingdom.

145

On that final day when Satan is released he will gather together those people on earth that choose darkness over light, evil over good, rebellion over obedience.

When the thousand years end, Satan will be let out of his prison. He will go out to deceive the nations from every corner of the earth, which are called Gog and Magog. He will gather them together for battle- a mighty host, as numberless as sand along the shore. And I saw them as they went up on the broad plain of the earth and surrounded God's people and the beloved city. But fire from heaven came down on the attacking armies and consumed them. Then the Devil, who betrayed them, was thrown into the lake of fire that burns with sulfur, joining the beast and the false prophet. There they will be tormented day and night forever and ever. (Revelation 20:7-10)

After one thousand years in prison Satan does not seek forgiveness from God. He will not repent from his wickedness and will have no sorrow, no remorse and no regrets. He will use this final opportunity to deceive those who do not love God and are not committed to serving Him. God will have zero tolerance for this final rebellion, no mercy and no "second chances". The final revolt of Satan and sinful man will be over in a flash of fire. Satan is a truly defeated foe, and his ultimate destiny is certain along with the doom of all who follow him. Satan is a created being that is powerless before God and will end up in the Lake of Fire forever and ever – never to bother, harm or tempt humans again!

The Final Judgment

The Great White Throne Judgment is a trial that will take place at the end of the thousand year reign of Jesus Christ. This court is specifically for all people who have rejected God's call to salvation. Every person who has refused to accept God's way to redemption from sin, will stand before their Creator and acknowledge that He is God-that Jesus is Lord. This horrifying judgment against sin is the most disturbing event in all of history because each person will be cast into the Lake of Fire, which will be their place throughout eternity.

And I saw a great white throne, and I saw the one who was sitting on it. The earth and sky fled from his presence, but they found no place to hide. I saw the dead, both great and small, standing before God's throne. And the books were opened, including the Book of Life. And the dead were judged according to the things written in the books, according to what they had done. (Revelation 20: 11-12)

God has two sets of books that serve as the divine records of the destiny of all human beings. First, there is the Book of Life, which contains the name of every person who will live out eternity with God. Then, there is the book that contains every word, thought and deed of the unredeemed dead. This book contains the evil works of the dead that will be resurrected to stand before their Creator at the Great White Throne. God will first look for their names in the Book of Life. When the name is not registered there, He will then open up the other book. Each one will be judged according to their works and then will be cast into the lake of fire. The entire human race will now be in a resurrected state either for eternity with God or apart from God forever. This is the final righteous judgement of good and evil. By this righteous judgment, God's absolute sovereignty will be manifested.

Death and Hades, the state of disembodied tormented existence, will also be thrown into the lake of fire. This is the second death, which is eternal separation from God. Jesus must reign until He has put all enemies under His feet and the last enemy to be destroyed is death. Following His destroying all dominion, authority and power of the persons and evil forces that oppose Him, Jesus will hand over the Kingdom to God.

He counts the stars and calls them all by name.
How great is our Lord! His power is absolute! His
understanding is beyond comprehension!

(Psalm 147:4-5)

Chapter Thirteen

INTO ETERNITY

After the Great White Throne Judgment a new earth and a new heaven will be created for the first heaven and the first earth will pass away. The New Jerusalem will descend, coming down out of heaven with God's throne. All redeemed people will rejoice forever in what God has created, for it will be a great delight with abundant joy and peace.

Then I saw a new heaven and a new earth, for the old heaven and the old earth had disappeared. And the sea was also gone. And I saw the holy city, the New Jerusalem, coming down from God out of heaven like a bride beautifully dressed for her husband. I heard a loud shout from the throne, saying, "Look, God's home is now among his people! He will live with them, and they will be his people. God himself will be with them He will wipe every tear from their eyes, and there will be no more death or sorrow or crying or pain. All these things are gone forever." (Revelation 21:1-4)

The world has never known the lights of a City so bright the glow from it lights up the earth both day and night. Its brilliance is like that of very rare and precious jewels, like a jasper and clear as crystal. It has a massive high wall with twelve gates and twelve angels stationed at the gates. On the gates are the names of the twelve tribes of Israel. There are three gates on the eastside, three gates on the north side, three gates on the south side and three gates on the west- side. The city is laid out like a square, its length being the same as its width and its height. The foundations of the city walls are made using precious stones and on them are the names of the twelve apostles of Jesus. The first foundation is jasper, the second sapphire, the third white agate, the fourth emerald, the fifth sardonyx, the sixth carnelian, the seventh chrysolite, the eighth beryl, the ninth topaz, the tenth chrysoprase, the eleventh jacinth, and the twelfth amethyst. The twelve gates are twelve pearls; each separate gate made of a single pearl. The main street of the city is of pure gold and is translucent like glass.

There is no temple in the city, for the Lord God Himself and Jesus are its temple. This city does not need the sun or the moon to give it light, for the splendor and the glory of God gives the light.

The gates of God's city shall never be shut. Nothing im-pure will ever enter it, nor will anyone who refuses God's love and plan. Only those whose names are written in the Lamb's Book of Life will inhabit this city.

There is a river whose water gives life, sparkling like crystal, flowing from the throne of God down into the middle of the great street of the city. On each side of the river stands the tree of life, with its twelve varieties of fruit, yielding fresh crops every month. The leaves of the tree are for the healing and the restoration of the nations.

No eye has seen, no ear has heard, and no mind has imagined
what God has prepared for those who love him.
(I Corinthians 2:9)

Prophecy is the lens given to mankind revealing the sovereign plans for the ages. These plans were set in place before time began. His love, grace and mercy has endured throughout the ages! The intricate design and profound strategy of His plans has secured our eternal inheritance. Even Angels long to see these things.

Christ is the one through whom God created
everything in heaven and earth. He made the things we
can see and the things we can't see- kings, kingdoms,
rulers, and authorities. Everything has been created through
him and for him. He existed before everything else began,
and he holds all creation together.

(Colossians 1: 16-17)

EPILOGUE

W e are finished reading the story of mankind: where we came from, where we are now, and what will happen in the future. We gather to hear it often so that we will not go astray and miss out on our eternal inheritance. Seal these truths in your heart and teach them to your children. Have your children tell it to their children, and their children to the future generations.

We find ourselves in a perpetual battleground, a Battle of the Ages. This war began back in heaven when Satan made his decision to battle against God to the death. It has continued throughout the ages and will not be over until Satan's release at the end of this millennial age. He will make his last stand, and there will be a fierce battle with Satan and his principalities of darkness when they are released from the pit. The Word says they will gather the last of us who will turn away from God, and choose to spend eternity with the spiritual forces of evil in the lake of fire, the place of everlasting torment.

Remember how easily the human race is deceived and tempted by their sin nature and always strive to be transformed from the old sin nature by the renewing of your mind through the Word of God, becoming partakers of the divine nature of Christ. Our victory is through our risen Savior, Jesus Christ!

The Creator of mankind does have an incredible master plan and purpose for humanity and He has revealed it through the inspired written scriptures. God has designed this marvelous redemptive plan which spans all of human history. The time and dates God has set by His own authority have been revealed to us by prophets and recorded in the Bible. The end result of this amazing plan is that He is bringing all His children home to live and reign with Him for eternity in the most incredibly fantastic place imaginable. This awesome destiny is available to all those who make a choice to love Him and receive His unconditional love. We have each been given a choice to serve God or Satan and that decision will determine where we will spend eternity.

He has left that choice entirely up to you.

The crowd is quiet. It is getting dark as the fire has begun to fade away. The annual reading of God's plan for mankind is over. As we all begin our journey home there is new revelation concerning life, eternity and God.

If there is anyone reading this account that has not personally received Jesus Christ as your Savior, trusting Him for your salvation now is the time! If you have never taken that step of faith or if you are unsure about your relationship with Christ, turn to him today and ask Jesus to come into your heart by faith. It is simple just pray this prayer:

Dear heavenly Father, I know that You have a plan for my life, because You created me and You love me. You created the Kingdom of heaven to be my eternal home with You. Forgive me of all my sins, failures, and my past. I believe the blood of your Son, Jesus, cleanses me from all sin. I repent of my sins and invite You, Jesus, to come into my heart and be my personal Savior. I trust that you are my Savior. Thank You for saving me according to what the Bible tells me "whoever calls on the Lord shall be saved." **Amen!**

And now, all glory to God, who is able to keep
you from stumbling, and who will bring you into his
glorious presence innocent of sin and with great joy. All glory
to him, who alone is god our Savior, through Jesus Christ our
Lord. Yes, glory, majesty, power, and authority belong to him,
in the beginning, now, and forevermore. Amen.

(Jude 14:24-25)

Messianic Prophecy:
Fulfillment by Jesus Christ

Messianic prophecy was fulfilled by the Messiah, Jesus Christ. Although many Jews did not accept Jesus as their Messiah, many did, and they became the Jewish sect later known as the Christians. Christianity, based in dramatic part on the fulfillment of historical prophecy, spread rapidly throughout the Roman Empire of the 1st Century. Examine the prophecies yourself, and calculate the probability of one man fulfilling just a handful of the most specific ones, and you'll be amazed.

Then Jesus said, "When I was with you before, I told you that everything written about me by Moses and the prophets and in the Psalms must all come true." Luke 24:44

The Old Testament verses are the prophecy; the New Testament verses proclaim the fulfillment. Check them all out for yourself!

- Born of a virgin (Isaiah 7:14; Matthew 1:21-23)
- A descendant of Abraham (Genesis 12:1-3; 22:18; Matthew 1:1; Galatians 3:16)
- Of the tribe of Judah (Genesis 49:10; Luke 3:23, 33; Hebrews 7:14)
- Of the house of David (2 Samuel 7:12-16; Matthew 1:1)

- Born in Bethlehem (Micah 5:2, Matthew 2:1; Luke 2:4-7)
- Taken to Egypt (Hosea 11:1; Matthew 2:14-15)
- Herod's killing of the infants (Jeremiah 31:15; Matthew 2:16-18)
- Anointed by the Holy Spirit (Isaiah 11:2; Matthew 3:16-17)
- Heralded by the messenger of the Lord (John the Baptist) (Isaiah 40:3-5; Malachi 3:1; Matthew 3:1-3)
- Would perform miracles (Isaiah 35:5-6; Matthew 9:35)
- Would preach good news (Isaiah 61:1; Luke 4:14-21)
- Would minister in Galilee (Isaiah 9:1; Matthew 4:12-16) Would cleanse the Temple (Malachi 3:1; Matthew 21:12-13)
- Would first present Himself as King 173,880 days from the decree to rebuild Jerusalem (Daniel 9:25; Matthew 21:4-11)
- Would enter Jerusalem as a king on a donkey (Zechariah 9:9; Matthew 21:4-9)
- Would be rejected by Jews (Psalm 118:22; I Peter 2:7)
- Die a humiliating death (Psalm 22; Isaiah 53) involving:
  1. rejection (Isaiah 53:3; John 1:10-11; 7:5,48)
  2. betrayal by a friend (Psalm 41:9; Luke 22:3-4; John 13:18)
  3. sold for 30 pieces of silver (Zechariah 11:12; Matthew 26:14-15)
  4. silence before His accusers (Isaiah 53:7; Matthew 27:12-14)
  5. being mocked (Psalm 22: 7-8; Matthew 27:31)
  6. beaten (Isaiah 52:14; Matthew 27:26)
  7. spit upon (Isaiah 50:6; Matthew 27:30)
  8. piercing His hands and feet (Psalm 22:16; Matthew 27:31)

9. being crucified with thieves (Isaiah 53:12; Matthew 27:38)

10. praying for His persecutors (Isaiah 53:12; Luke 23:34)

11. piercing His side (Zechariah 12:10; John 19:34)

12. given gall and vinegar to drink (Psalm 69:21, Matthew 27:34, Luke 23:36)

13. no broken bones (Psalm 34:20; John 19:32-36)

14. buried in a rich man's tomb (Isaiah 53:9; Matthew 27:57-60)

15. casting lots for His garments (Psalm 22:18; John 19:23-24)

16. Would rise from the dead!! (Psalm 16:10; Mark 16:6; Acts 2:31)

- Ascend into Heaven (Psalm 68:18; Acts 1:9)
- Would sit down at the right hand of God (Psalm 110:1; Hebrews 1:3)

Messianic Prophecy -
What Are The Odds of Fulfillment Without God?

Messianic Prophecy is so powerful because of the statistical odds that one man would fulfill every single one of them. If we just analyze seven of the more specific prophecies in the Old Testament, that were later fulfilled in the Person of Jesus Christ, we are stunned by the statistical impossibility of such an historical reality. As an illustration, we have inserted some conservative "odds" alongside seven established prophecies.

Please feel free to propose your own prophecies and your own odds - the dramatic point will still be made!

Messianic Prophecy	Odds Without God
1. Jesus would be a descendant of David.	10^4 (1 in 10,000)
2. Jesus would be born in Bethlehem.	10^5 (1 in 100,000)
3. Jesus would be a miracle worker.	10^5 (1 in 100,000)
4. Jesus would present Himself as a King riding on a donkey	10^6 (1 in 1,000,000)
5. Jesus would be betrayed by a friend for 30 pieces of silver.	10^6 (1 in 1,000,000)
6. Jesus would be crucified.	10^6 (1 in 1,000,000)
7. Jesus would first present Himself as King 173,880 days from the decree of Artaxerxes to rebuild Jerusalem.	10^6 (1 in 1,000,000)
Total Probability (without God)	10^{38} (1 in 100 billion, billion, billion, billion)

Messianic Prophecy - The Challenge

Messianic prophecy is phenomenal evidence that sets the Bible apart from the other "holy books." We strongly encourage you to read the Old Testament prophecies and the New Testament fulfillments on the previous page. Better yet, get a Jewish Tanakh (the Hebrew scripture read in the Jewish synagogues) and read the Messianic prophecies from there. It is dramatic, eye-opening and potentially life-changing!

Messianic prophecy compilation provided by www.allabouttruth.org

Prophecies Describing the Second Coming of Jesus Christ

Perhaps the most anticipated event in the world is the Second Coming of Jesus Christ. Both the Old and New Testament are filled with multitudes of prophecies describing his return to earth. He will rule and reign over all the earth from Jerusalem. This thousand year age, known as the Millennial reign of Christ, is described as a time when righteousness and justice will prevail. There will be great peace and harmony unlike humans have yet experienced on earth. Many prophecies describe the second coming in great detail.

Jesus Himself promised, "And then at last, the sign of the coming of the Son of Man will appear in the heavens, and there will be deep mourning among all the nations of the earth. And they will see the Son of Man arrive on the clouds of heaven with power and great glory. (Matthew 24:30). For I, the Son of Man, will come in the glory of my Father with his angels and will judge all people according to their deeds. (Matthew 16:27)

This is a partial list of prophecies about the second coming of Jesus Christ:

- "When the Son of Man returns, it will be like it was in Noah's day. (Matthew 24:27)

- ...when the Son of Man comes in his glory...then he will sit upon his glorious throne. (Matthew 25:31)
- ...in the future you will see me, the Son of Man ...coming back on the clouds of heaven. (Matthew 26:64)
- ...when I return in the glory of my Father with the holy angels. (Mark 8:38)
- Then everyone will see the Son of Man arrive on the clouds with great power... (Mark 13:26)
- Yes, it will be 'business as usual' right up to the hour when the Son of Man returns. (Luke 17: 30)
- But when I, the Son of Man, return, how many will I find who have faith? (Luke 18:8)
- "And there will be strange events in the skies-signs in the sun, moon, and stars. And down here on earth the nations will be in turmoil, perplexed by the roaring seas and strange tides. Then everyone will see the Son of Man arrive on the clouds with power and great glory. (Luke 21: 25, 27)
- When everything is ready, I will come and get you, so that you will always be with me where I am. (John 14:3)
- Jesus has been taken away from you into heaven. And someday just as you saw him go, he will return! (Acts. 1:11)
- ...he will send Jesus your Messiah to you again. (Acts 3:20)
- 'Afterward I will return, and I will restore the fallen kingdom of David.' (Acts 15:16)

- ...eagerly wait for the return of our Lord Jesus Christ. (I Corinthians 1:7)
- When the Lord comes, he will bring our deepest secrets to light and will reveal our private motives. (I Corinthians 4:5)
- For every time you eat this bread and drink this cup, you are announcing the Lord's death until he comes again. (I Corinthians 11:26)
- But there is an order to this resurrection: Christ was raised first: then when Christ comes back, all his people will be raised. (I Corinthians 15:23)
- For I want you to understand what really matters, so that you may live pure and blameless lives until Christ returns. (Philippians 1:10)
- And we are eagerly waiting for him to return as our Savior. (Philippians 3:20)
- And they speak of how you are looking forward to the coming of God's Son from heaven-Jesus, whom God raised from the dead. (1 Thessalonians 1:10)
- ...as we stand together before our Lord Jesus when he comes back again. (1 Thessalonians 2:19)
- ...when you stand before God our Father on that day when our Lord Jesus comes with all those who belong to him. (1 Thessalonians 3:13)
- We who are still living when the Lord returns... For the Lord himself will come down from heaven with a commanding shout, with the call of the archangel, and with the trumpet call of God. (1 Thessalonians 4:15-16)

- ...and may your whole spirit and soul and body be kept blameless until that day when our Lord Jesus Christ comes again. (1 Thessalonians 5:23)
- And God will provide rest for you who are being persecuted and also for us when the Lord Jesus appears from heaven. He will come with his mighty angels (2 Thessalonians 1:7)
- When he comes to receive glory and praise from his holy people. (2 Thessalonians 1:10)
- And now, brothers and sister, let us tell you about the coming again of our Lord Jesus Christ and how we will be gathered together to meet him. (2 Thessalonians 2:1)
- ...obey his commands with all purity. Then no one can find fault with you from now until our Lord Jesus Christ returns. (1 Timothy 6:14)
- ...Christ Jesus-who will someday judge the living and the dead when he appears to set up his Kingdom: (2 Timothy 4:1)
- And now the prize awaits me-the crown of righteousness what the Lord, the righteous Judge, will give me on that great day of his return. (2 Timothy 4:8)
- So also Christ died only once as a sacrifice to take away the sins of many people. He will come again but not to deal with our sins again. (Hebrews 9:28)
- And let us not neglect our meeting together, as some people do, but encourage and warn each other, especially now that the day of his coming back again is drawing near. (Hebrews 10:25)

- …you must be patient as you wait for the Lord's return. (James 5:7)
- So think clearly and exercise self-control. Look forward to the special blessings that will come to you at the return of Jesus Christ. (1 Peter 1:13)
- And when the head Shepherd comes, your reward will be a never-ending share in his glory and honor. (1 Peter 5:4)
- For we were not making up clever stories when we told you about the power of our Lord Jesus Christ and his coming again. (2 Peter 1:16)
- …in the last days there will be scoffers who will laugh at the truth and do every evil thing they desire. This will be their argument; "Jesus promised to come back, did he? (2 Peter 3: 3-4)
- The Lord isn't really being slow about his promise to return, as some people think. No, he is being patient for your sake. (2 Peter 3:9)
- …continue to live in fellowship with Christ so that when he returns, you will be full of courage and not shrink back from him in shame. (1 John 2: 28)
- Yes, dear friends, we are already God's children, and we can't even imagine what we will be like when Christ returns. (1 John 3: 2)
- Grace and peace from the one who is, who always was, and who is still to come (Revelation 1:4)
- Look! He comes with the clouds of heaven. And everyone will see him-even those who pierced him. (Revelation 1:7)
- Look, I am coming quickly. (Revelation 3:11)

- "Take note; I will come as unexpectedly as a thief! Blessed are all who are watching for me..." (Revelation 16:15)
- "See, I am coming soon, and my reward is with me, to repay all according to their deeds. (Revelation 22:12)
- He who is the faithful witness to all these things says, "Yes, I am coming soon!" (Revelation 22:20)
- He is coming to judge the earth. He will judge the world with righteousness and all the nations with his truth. (Psalm 96:13)
- The heavens declare his righteousness; every nation sees his glory. (Psalm 97:6)
- For the Lord will rebuild Jerusalem. He will appear in his glory. (Psalm 102:16)
- The Lord Almighty will hover over Jerusalem as a bird hovers around its nest. He will defend and save the city; he will pass over it and rescue it." (Isaiah 31:5)
- Yes, the Sovereign Lord is coming in all his glorious power. He will rule with awesome strength. (Isaiah 40: 10)
- "The Redeemer will come to Jerusalem," says the Lord...(Isaiah 59:20)
- The Sovereign Lord will show his justice to the nations of the world. (Isaiah 61: 11)
- The Lord has sent this message to every land: "Tell the people of Israel, 'Look, your Savior is coming...And Jerusalem will be known as the Desirable Place and the City No Longer Forsaken. (Isaiah 62:11-12)

- See, the Lord is coming with fire, and his swift chariots of destruction roar like a whirlwind. (Isaiah 66:15)
- ...for I am coming to live among you. Many nations will join themselves to the Lord on that day, and they too will be my people. I will live among you, and you will know that the Lord Almighty sent me to you. ...and he will once again choose Jerusalem to be his own city. (Zechariah 2:10-12)
- I am returning to Mount Zion, and I will live in Jerusalem. Then Jerusalem will be called the Faithful City...(Zechariah 8:3)
- Your king will bring peace to the nations. His realm will stretch from sea to sea and from the Euphrates River to the ends of the earth. (Zechariah 9:10)
- And the Lord will be king over all the earth. (Zechariah 14:9)

The Seven Thousand Year Plan of God

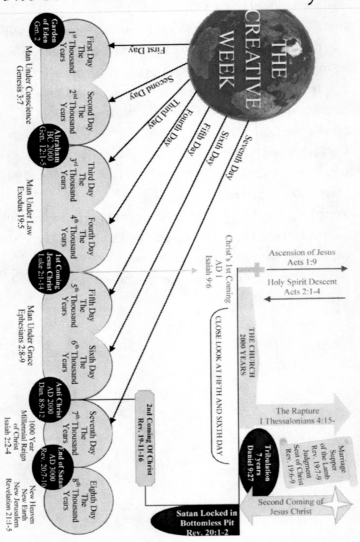

References

1. Billy Graham, *Angels* (Dallas, Texas: Word Publishing, 1994).

2. Hugh Ross, *The Fingerprint of God* (Orange, California: Promise Publishing Co., 1991).

3. John Hagee, *Beginning of the End* (Nashville, Tennessee: Thomas Nelson Publishers, 1996).

4. John Hagee, *Prophecy Study Bible* (Nashville, Tennessee: Thomas Nelson Publishers, 1997).

5. John Walvoord, *Armageddon, Oil and the Middle East Crisis* (Grand Rapids, Michigan: Zondervan Publishing House, 1990).

6. Lester Sumrall, *Demonology and Deliverance, Principalities and Powers Volume 2* (South Bend, Indiana: LeSea Publishing Company, 1995).

7. Lester Sumrall, *The Gifts and Ministries of the Holy Spirit* (South Bend Indiana: LeSea Publishing Company, 1992).

8. J. Dwight Pentecost, *Things to Come* (Grand Rapids, Michigan: Zondervan Publishing House, 1958).

9. Herbert Lockyear, *All the Doctines of the Bible* (Grand Rapids, Michigan: Zondervan Publishing House, 1964).

10. Finis Jennings Dake, *The Dake Annotated Reference Bible* (Lawrenceville, Georgia: Dake Bible Sales, Incl, 1968).

CPSIA information can be obtained at www.ICGtesting.com
Printed in the USA
LVOW062128290212

271087LV00001B/55/P